Human Rights, Security Politics and Embodiment

Human Rights, Security Politics and Embodiment

Aneira J. Edmunds

ANTHEM PRESS

Anthem Press
An imprint of Wimbledon Publishing Company
www.anthempress.com

This edition first published in UK and USA 2023
by ANTHEM PRESS
75–76 Blackfriars Road, London SE1 8HA, UK
or PO Box 9779, London SW19 7ZG, UK
and
244 Madison Ave #116, New York, NY 10016, USA

British Library Cataloguing-in-Publication Data
A catalogue record for this book is available from the British Library.

Library of Congress Cataloging-in-Publication Data: 2023943065
A catalog record for this book has been requested.

ISBN-13: 978-1-83998-447-1 (Pbk)
ISBN-10: 1-83998-447-3 (Pbk)

This title is also available as an e-book.

For Josephine whose kindness, intelligence, wit and humour have been invaluable to me and everyone who knows her. And to Sam, for being her rock.

The Cemetery of the Companionless in Kilyos is a real place. It is growing fast. Lately, an increasing number of refugees who drowned in the Aegean Sea while trying to cross to Europe have been buried here. Like all other graves, theirs have only numbers, rarely names. Elif Shafak, *Ten Minutes and 38 Seconds in This Strange World.*

What part of my body do you want me to give to demonstrate the effort of provoking the humanity in you?[1] Grenfell Survivor.

1 Quoted in Stonebridge (2021: 74).

CONTENTS

ACKNOWLEDGEMENTS

I would like to acknowledge Professor Bryan S. Turner, whose work has been a critical inspiration for me, always the innovator. Nor can I thank more highly the team at Anthem; all of whom have been considerate, supportive and creative and allowed me the time I needed.

INTRODUCTION: AN OUTLINE

Theories of securitisation have been indispensable in shedding light on how governmental security politics operate through discourses or institutions. Key theorists have noted their state-centredness, but they have yet to remedy this. The focus on the state, moreover, has led to a neglect of how virtuous bodies, supra-national bodies, might become mixed up in security politics. This book takes the rare step of applying such theories to supra-national organisations and politics and, importantly, allegedly virtuous ones: judicial human rights in Europe and, to a lesser extent, other regions. It explores how such human rights organisations, devoted to holding state power in check, might be complicit in governmental security agendas to the extent of losing their role as neutral arbiters of state actions to involvement in state-led security politics and, therefore, contributing to the demise of their own animus: the protection of bodily vulnerability. It links the socio-legal study of human rights with the politics of securitisation and with European Studies, re-appraising the aspect of the European Project that anticipated closer harmonisation and integration of nation-states through the operation of supra-national courts like the European Court of Human Rights (ECtHR).

It begins by contemplating the relationship between human rights, embodiment and vulnerability and seeks to foreground the body in human rights. Then it moves on to demonstrate and explain the subordination of international rights to national security through the question of embodiment, the most fundamental of human rights being to protect bodily integrity. When the human body has become an object of securitisation, for example in relation to the veiled woman, where have judicial human rights in Europe stood? While non-governmental human rights organisations have lobbied against repeated bans on the veil by various European countries, without evidence and with deference to states' ownership of security matters, the ECtHR has contributed to the precarity of veiled Muslim women – signaling a failure to denounce gender-based violence. This is contrasted with the United States, which allows public veiling, but whose destruction of bodily integrity in the name of security has been manifest in other ways, most obviously in Abu Ghraib and Guantanamo Bay.

My aim is to tease out the contextual background to the way women's bodies (and to a lesser extent, men's) have been treated by judicial human rights. I show that the steady expansion – in democratic countries – of laws restricting women's dress and conduct, and [Muslim] women's lack of success in contesting this via the national or supra-national judiciary, stem partly from the liberal individualism that has characterised human rights from their inception. Legal arguments framed around individual human rights have led to an appearance of judiciaries buying into old orientalist and colonialist tropes about the exotic, dangerous, covered woman. Moreover, these narratives are given extra credence through governance feminism, which routinely brings out the right kind of Muslim woman – exposed – to critique its opponents, raising the question of how there can be a meeting between governance and post-colonial feminism. Further, we see that, in an age of European populism, even those institutions supposedly beyond such impulses, are caught up in it and the existential crises raised by populist politics.

This analysis, drawn from theoretical debates over human rights and securitisation and the reality of legal cases and judgements in an interdisciplinary way, shows why the Muslim woman's body has become the site of political and legal battles disproportionate to the number of Muslim women who cover and especially a small subset who wear full veils in Europe. Growing concerns about security provide practical arguments about the need for faces to be kept visible and opportunities for concealed weaponry to be minimised. But these have been eclipsed in significance by intellectual arguments concerning the exercise of civil rights, and visible tokens of its possible curtailment. European-generated concepts of freedom and gender equality have fuelled the legal argument that conformity to strict, prescribed dress rules indicates hidden coercion, an observable restriction of the body which indicates an otherwise unobservable restriction of the mind.

Chapter 1 argues that the body must be foregrounded in human rights because their very essence is to offer us protection of our bodily integrity based on inherent frailty and vulnerability that we all share. This vision, however, has been disfigured as we acknowledge that warfare, conflict and associated regimes of control have shown up the limits of such bodily rights, often in brutal ways – most obviously torture and disappearances – associated with states of control, typically driven by nationalistic impulses. While the body, with its vulnerability to disease, ageing and death, stands at the centre of human rights, bodies are differentially treated. The value of bodies is, moreover, unevenly distributed as some sit at the top of humanity's hierarchy and others are relegated to the bottom, subjected to torture, detention or washed up on the shores of the Mediterranean, as growing numbers of people are migrating to escape conflict or other threats such as climate change.

Nationalistic biopolitics are also sexed so that women's reproductive capacity is targeted through rape camps and other practises aimed at subjecting women's bodies to forms of being cast out of politics. Throughout history, and with human rights looking on, the vulnerability of the body has been repeatedly abused and subjected to securitising measures which have not been harnessed by judicial human rights whose ultimate deference is to national sovereignty. Moreover, bodily vulnerability is not simply material, so it is also essential to look at dress as inherent to embodiment because it is through dress that we convey our universal human inclination towards expressing our inner identity. Dress is a second skin and, as such, should also be at the centre of human rights' protections. Human rights therefore must not only restrict themselves to protection from physical violations but also from bodily violations that include prohibitions on dress, especially religious dress. The chapter signposts the reader towards how the securitisation of bodies and bodily dispositions needs to move away from its state-centredness to address how such violations also happen under the auspices of the most virtuous and supra-national of organisations such as human rights courts.

Chapter 2 looks at the contribution of securitisation theory to shedding light on the ways bodies are controlled and regulated. Theories of securitisation[1] have been indispensable in exposing how governmental security politics operate through discourses or institutions and how this work is especially relevant to understanding how control regimes regulate the body. While this work has made a compelling contribution to the field, it has been limited by its Euro- and state-centred focus and neglect of transnational, particularly virtuous institutions, such as human rights ones. By expanding the theory's concept of audience, this chapter suggests that non-state institutions may lose their role as neutral audience and arbiter of security politics and, rather, become embroiled in them. It will also suggest that by sidelining gendered and racialised forms of security and by centring its theory on the state, it leaves scope for an innovative angle by exploring how security politics might operate through virtuous supra-national institutions and how securitisation renders some groups precarious and vulnerable and how this works through racial and gender domination within judicial human rights, the supposed checks on nation-states. It demonstrates and explains the subordination of international rights to national security through the question of embodiment, the

---

1 Securitisation theory is vast and ever-evolving. There are three schools of thought associated with it: the Paris School, the Copenhagen School and the Aberystwyth School. Distinct in many ways, there are overlaps between these different branches of the theory. It is not my intention to provide an exhaustive account of the different schools.

most fundamental of human rights being to protect bodily integrity. When the human body has become an object of securitisation, for example in relation to the veiled woman, where have judicial human rights in Europe stood? While non-governmental human rights organisations have lobbied against repeated bans on the veil by various European countries, without evidence and with deference to states' ownership of security matters, the ECtHR has contributed to the precarity of veiled Muslim women – signaling a failure to denounce gender-based violence. This is contrasted with the United States, which allows public veiling, but whose destruction of bodily integrity in the name of security has been manifest in other ways, most obviously in Abu Ghraib and Guantanamo Bay – putting their resources into hard rather than soft securitisation measures.

Chapter 3 looks more closely at the ECtHR's treatment of strategic litigation taken by the veiled Muslim woman in Europe. It claims that the court's commitment to embodied integrity (central to human rights) has been undermined by its deference to the nation-state over questions of security. The result has been that key institutions, which should be acting transnationally to protect Muslim women, have contributed to their precarity by sanctioning, if only implicitly, extreme practises such as stripping Muslim women of their coverings in public. Moreover, it suggests that a major reason for this is that judicial human rights buy into the ideal of the liberated, female body as an exposed one and that the ECtHR has itself engaged in efforts to domesticate the disruptive figure of the veiled woman, viewed contradictorily as both dangerous and passive. The aim is to tease out the contextual background to how (mainly) women's bodies have been treated by judicial human rights. I show that the steady expansion – in democratic countries – of laws restricting women's dress and conduct, and Muslim women's lack of success in contesting this via the national or supra-national judiciary, stem partly from the liberal individualism that has characterised human rights from their inception. Legal arguments framed around individual human rights have led to an appearance of judiciaries buying into old orientalist and colonialist tropes about the exotic, dangerous, covered woman. Moreover, these narratives are given extra credence through liberal feminism, which routinely displays the right kind of Muslim woman – exposed – to critique its opponents, raising the question of how there can be a meeting between Western, liberal feminism and post-colonial feminism. Further, we see that, in an age of European populism, even those institutions supposedly beyond such impulses, are caught up in it and the existential crises raised by populist politics with which Western, liberal feminism has aligned itself. The Muslim woman's body has become the site of political and legal battles disproportionate to the number of Muslim women who cover and an especially small subset who wear full covering in Europe. Growing concerns about security provide practical arguments about the need for faces to be kept visible and opportunities for concealed weaponry to be minimised. But these have been eclipsed by intellectual arguments concerning the exercise of civil rights, and visible tokens of its possible curtailment. European-generated concepts of freedom and gender equality have fuelled the legal argument that conformity to strict, prescribed dress rules indicates hidden coercion, an observable restriction of the body which indicates an otherwise unobservable restriction of the mind. With such embedded stereotypical notions about the veiled Muslim woman's body and the failure of strategic litigation by covered Muslim women, it is hard to imagine how stigmatised women can win the right not to assimilate in the European public sphere.

Chapter 4 offers a wide exploration of why an institution, supposedly committed to protecting bodily integrity, has failed to do so. It will argue that the ECtHR's judgements on Muslim veiling show up the limits of citizenship, the failure of human rights to trump national citizenship and being caught up in the rise of right-wing populist politics across Europe and enabled to do so because human rights remain entrenched in neo-liberal individualism and age-old colonial legacies. This provides further evidence that the triumphalism of the 1990s which heralded the West's ownership of human rights was misplaced as subsequent events revealed the limits to Western human rights. Rights, far from spreading inexorably across the globe, have gone into retreat. It will look further at debates within feminism, which have seen it divide to the extent that liberal feminism finds itself in the company of the populists. It will address how this schism can be overcome to enable solidarity within feminism about human rights and the woman's body.

The final chapter, the conclusion, signposts the reader towards an answer to how can human rights protect people from the infringement of their bodily integrity and vulnerability. It is devoted to creatively constructing a possible strategy for desecuritising judicial human rights to enable them to fulfil their basic normative function – namely protecting material bodily integrity and symbolic bodily integrity in the public sphere. I argue for women coming together in a politics of rights type of activism allied with a rebellious cosmopolitanism that allows them to reconfigure the public sphere and end the division between feminist movements, forcing judicial human rights to respond to the varied visible politics in the public sphere and, ultimately, overcome its conservatism that leads it to comply with ideas about dangerous bodies at times of heightened national security. While recognising the limits and failures of human rights, which are significant, the book ends on an optimistic note and suggests that our scepticism about judicial rights is justified but that we need to avoid a nihilistic approach. Alongside our caution, the project of rescuing judicial human rights from the constraints that prevent them from foregrounding the protection of bodily vulnerability, physical or material, should start by harnessing a combination of a politics of rights and rebellious cosmopolitanism (in the spirit of Camus) that involves using the public sphere and public spaces as an arena for turning bodily vulnerability into resistance. The forms of mobilisation may be multiple but need to forge bridges across differences and an openness to strangers that is formed through rebellion. Such rebellion will involve protests against bans on dress, forging alliances with other vulnerable bodies, beating populism through protest and ending the schism within feminism where women are attacking women. Protesting through covering and uncovering is one of the key answers to the question of the veil so that choice is re-centred without name-calling – which has characterised the debates about women's spaces. Mutual recognition and compromise, starting from the ground to combat the top-down bureaucratic apparatus of human rights, will be essential in saving them.

Chapter 1

SOCIOLOGY, HUMAN RIGHTS AND THE BODY

Despite the extensive literature from secular, Western feminism, the material body has been strangely marginalised. Yet, the reproductive capacity of women has been cruelly exploited in rape camps throughout history during warfare, designed to destroy biological continuity. There are multiple examples of this, as diverse as Japan's state-endorsed use of comfort women held in stations during its occupation of China in World War II; the use of sexualised violence by the Indonesian security forces as a form of land-grabbing in West Papua to dilute indigenous land rights; the mass rape of women in Bosnia to destroy religious identity and Muslim continuity; and modern-day Uyghurs in China where reports have shown that inside the country's re-education camps, women have been systematically raped and sexually abused (Ochab, 2021).[1] Rape has, moreover, become a weapon of war against asylum seekers in new border conflicts, across the world and including on the borders of western Europe (Fernandez, 2023).[2]

Post-democratic times have seen the rise of the global right – personified in populist leaders in North America, Latin America and Europe – which has created a revitalisation of neo-liberalism. Such developments have made life more precarious, and a democratic deficit has arisen out of greater precarity and securitisation, which has targeted vulnerable citizens and forms of embodiment considered unacceptable and subjected to excessive regulation (Sabsay, 2020). In contemporary secular Europe, it is the Muslim body that has become a site for vilification in a time of heightened national security and securitisation, which has turned the bearded man and the veiled[3] woman into

---

1 https://www.forbes.com/sites/ewelinaochab/2021/02/03/behind-the-camps-gates-rape-and-sexual-violence-against-uyghur-women/.

2 https://www.aljazeera.com/opinions/2023/3/19/rape-as-a-weapon-in-the-war-on-asylum-seekers.

3 I am using the term 'veil' or 'veiling' to incorporate the variety of forms of covering, from the hijab to the burka or the burkini.

suspect bodies. Controversies about veiling have traversed secular Europe, drawing attention to the vulnerability of Muslim women. Curiously, the politics of the veil has led to an unimagined alliance between security politics, human rights and Western liberal feminists whose opposition to the veil has led to complicity with reactionary populism – including the far right such as Marine Le Pen. The re-orientalisation of the Muslim woman's body has led human rights and feminism to ally themselves with securitisation and populism, and ultimately, objection to covering is rooted in the perception of sexual availability and therefore reproduction. These unlikely connections mean that human rights, instead of protecting Muslim women's bodily integrity, have succeeded in increasing their vulnerability. It is therefore critical that we overcome divisions within feminism that strengthen populism and the securitising of Muslim bodies so that judicial human rights halt their self-evident inability/unwillingness to protect bodily integrity essential to their foundation in deference to national security, to prevent the ongoing normalised misuse of (unwanted) bodily dispositions in the public sphere.

The problem is that sociology has sidelined human rights because of its commitment to universalism, which sits uneasily with the discipline's allegiance to cultural relativism. This orientation has led to a social constructionist bias within the discipline, which is especially pronounced when it comes to the body – to the extent that there has been a tendency to reject any bodily materiality. However, distancing oneself from reactionary biological determinism need not mean that there cannot be a meeting of minds if we adopt a weak rather than a strong cultural relativism that allows for intercultural dialogue and critique. Even those authors known for their advancement of the performative nature of the body acknowledge that it meets real limits (Butler, 1995). When thinking about human rights, security and the body, these tensions easily reach the surface, forcing us to consider the difficulties of overcoming them. The recent invention of multiple feminisms, in reaction to post-democracy, has created new possibilities for this (Sabsay, 2020).

The bias towards methodological nationalism (Beck, 2007) within the social sciences has also contributed to the subordination of universal rights in favour of a concentration mainly on national citizenship – that is, rights traditionally linked to state-building. While sociology has been preoccupied with the nation-state as the basic unit of analysis, it has overlooked universal analytical/methodological frameworks which suggest that citizenship rights could, potentially, be realised through non-national institutions such as the European Parliament or the European Court of Justice (ECJ) and, ideally, that human rights trump nationalistic rights by operating above the nation-state and beyond national governments. This analytical nationalism was challenged with globalisation, which led to a movement within social theory towards a more universal perspective on rights and concepts such as post-national citizenship that were not tied to the nation-state. In this context, it was argued that the creation of supra-national organisations such as the European Court of Human Rights (ECtHR) meant that rights claims could bypass national jurisdictions through direct access to judicial human rights (Turner, 1993; Soysal, 1995). Unfortunately, this optimism about the power of international human rights was precipitate.

A universal framework for rights, while avoiding the discredited natural rights tradition, has been proposed to circumvent intellectual constraints for dealing with human rights by foregrounding the body and specifically its inherent frailty and precarity caused by conditions of scarcity, disease, ageing and death as well as the precariousness of social institutions which everyone shared (Turner, 2006). This precariousness has been enhanced by new technological developments, which undermined security through cyber-attacks and biotechnology, and natural developments such as climate change and global pandemics which showed states up for their inability to reduce precarity and new forms of warfare which exposed the state's monopoly over violence and citizenship. Pandemics such as AIDS and SARS (now Covid) powerfully demonstrated our shared vulnerability and underlined the fact that we live in a somatic (corporeal) society where the body is increasingly managed by new surveillance regimes, leading to egregious transgressions of rights that include state control over reproduction or military use of the body. The risks of Artificial Intelligence (AI) are only now being addressed.

Foregrounding shared vulnerability is graphically illustrated in the worst forms of bodily violations where there is a total loss of autonomy and control, such as in genocide and torture. In torture, we see some of the cruellest of theatrical aspects of state control of the body, where it is turned into a plaything and the worst forms of brutality are inflicted on a powerless victim to prolong the pain and terrify others. It typically starts by stripping the victim naked, rendering them utterly vulnerable and powerless, and becomes a performative act. Torture's theatrical aspect is captured in how the spaces in which it takes place often have a cinematic element to them: the Production Room in the Philippines; The Cinema Room in Vietnam; and The Blue Lit Stage in Chile (Lazreg, 2016). The digital circulation of the images in Abu Ghraib – of naked men forced to engage in sexual acts – is a malevolent form of drama and malicious theatre (Eisenman, 2010).

So, a comprehensive understanding of human rights should centre the body as both real and constructed, and the tensions around this distinction can be resolved through the idea of shared bodily vulnerability. However, bodily precarity is unevenly distributed, and this book is precisely about how some bodies are more unsafe than others and are more likely to be cast out of judicial human rights protections than others through their role in securitisation; how some are more desired than others; and how some are unwanted and disposable in a way others are not. Vulnerability is gendered and racialised. Violence against women has not been included as a human rights violation in the way violence against men is. War rape, which is habitually used in ethnic or national cleansing, creating both personal trauma amongst innocent civilians and shame amongst those unable to protect women from this violation, is one of the most extreme displays of this. Male soldiers might be forced to take part as a rite of passage, with the threat of death or castration for refusing, with some of the most shocking cases involving holding women in camps where they are held and raped until they conceive and throughout the pregnancy, with Kosovo being one of the most recognised examples (Diken and Laustsen, 2005). This sexualised form of genocide attracted much attention after the Kosovan conflict, but it is a routine aspect of genocide and, significantly, this has historically been neglected by human rights as one of the most fundamental of violations (MacKinnon, 2007).

Control of bodies, moreover, cannot be separated from national domination, which is also gendered, as the nation is presented as male, but women are the source of its reproduction and racialised as some minorities are used as its antithesis. Nationalist projects in countries as diverse as the United States, China, Turkey and India expose how nations are sexed and how sexuality creates and sustains national identities, such that national belonging is gendered, with masculine traits being prized in the process of national building, but women are key to its reproduction (Mayer, 2000). Nationalist movements invariably rest on an ideal of the male: virile and strong. The strong, male body has been central to nationalist struggles and national well-being. For example, the Zionist movement between the two World Wars sought to create the ideal of the new Jew, whose youthfulness and dynamism contrasted with the supposed trait – of weakness – of past generations of Jews. It is in the image of the Ashkenazi Jew that Israel was formed, laying the foundation for (ongoing) divisions between Ashkenazi (European) Jews and Sephardi Jews (of Afro-Asian origin) who emigrated to Israel in the 1950s (Mayer, 2000). The body is central to power struggles, including geopolitical ones, and state control of bodies in general, but women and minorities in particular, throw light on how, during heightened nationalist conflict, there are gender-specific aspects of human rights violations (Bordo, 2004) and ethnic ones, such as the genocide of Rohingya Muslims in Myanmar.

National strife and conflict demand that those on opposing sides discipline their respective constituencies and enforce an unnatural homogeneity. This drive to dominate and control rebellious bodies is most visible during wars for national independence, and those fighting for independence as well as those fighting against it might enact the most brutal of practises to enforce conformity and loyalty. Commitment to human rights is abandoned, as we saw in France's brutal and barbaric practises against Algerians fighting for independence (Fanon, 2004 [1961]). Colonialism's capacity to dehumanise the enemy is transported into the metropole: French brutality in Algeria was imported into French territory when protesters against the war in Algeria were thrown into the Seine amidst chaos on the streets in the late 1960s, where students and workers stood with Algerians in their fight for liberation. This denigration of colonial subjects works at a micro level too, which Fanon (2021 [1952]) showed us in his observation on how structural racism in France impacted black identity through daily exposure to being judged and stigmatised because of the colour of one's skin. Societal views are internalised, he argued, creating a form of double containment so that free black people could not escape their own sense of containment as they watched the way others watched them and assumed their contempt and distaste. This observation informed Fanon's concept of the double bind, where even after decolonisation, those subjected to the denigration of being colonised suffered from crushing objecthood, that is, a hyper-corporeality, as they saw their own body in the third person (Mbembe, 2017).

The broad existential claim, namely, that everyone is precarious, does not imply that vulnerability is undifferentiated because it is also premised on the idea that our social existence depends on mutual support to avoid statelessness, homelessness, destitution and injustice, which are differentially distributed. Our precarity, while universally shared, also has a contingent quality and is differentiated (Sabsay, 2020). It depends on different organisational structures and the absence of supportive ones, which are unequally distributed. The general existential claim can, therefore, also be cast in specific ways. While this undermines equal bodily rights, it has the advantage of showing how precarity cannot be abstracted from politics that centre on the protection of bodily needs. It is our very interdependence and lack thereof that creates more fragile and vulnerable lives for some than others (Butler, 2012). In her novel, *Ten Minutes and 38 Seconds*, Elif Shafak (2020) vividly shows the reader how some bodies are more disposable than others by introducing her to the Graveyard of the Companionless in Istanbul, which buries the bodies of the unwanted: prostitutes, transwomen and asylum seekers, hidden in a site that is invisible to tourists and stripped of their names and identity, marked only by numbers and impossible to mourn.

While we might expect the law, especially human rights law, to be free from such prejudices, there is compelling evidence that it continues to discriminate against certain bodies, enhancing their vulnerability, especially in times of heightened national security. From their inception, human rights privileged the propertied, European male body. The normal body discards women's bodies, though the male body, while privileged, is only privileged to the extent it represents those who hold power. It is not possible, therefore, to see the body as a blank slate despite its materiality; bodies are sexed in social ways and most theories about the body have been written about and on the male body. Social theorists – such as Derrida – when talking about corporality, tend to have the male body in mind and neglect the bodily experiences of women (Grosz, 1994) and minorities. The differentiated way some bodies are cast out of human rights law and others are not, reveals the inequalities within human rights law. Currently concerning is the move towards quasi-embodiment, where corporate entities are given legal status alongside the universal commitment to protecting universal embodiment, with the effect of intensifying rather than overcoming bodily vulnerability. This liberal view of the body (or quasi-body) has begun to impact human rights law so that bodies outside of model ones – women, asylum seekers and minorities – are denied protection, a development that risks a return to prioritising the white, propertied male (Grear, 2006).

Centring the human body – real and constructed – resists the trend towards giving non-embodied institutions legal personhood. Human and non-human legal rights cannot be conflated because to do so would give rights to powerful non-human bodies such as corporations and allow capitalism to colonise human rights. We need to protect human rights from this trend towards protecting the collective right of global capital to justify corporate welfare even if, by doing so, rights violations are carried out. It is critical to resist this corporate colonisation of rights whose institutions may stimulate growth and hence generalised well-being. Failure to challenge the idea of corporations having fundamental rights may ultimately lead to a complete overhaul of human rights' foundational vision to reach and protect human welfare, albeit social, economic or physical, so that vulnerable groups are protected somehow if not by their governments (Baxi, 2009). Ultimately, corporations cannot feel pain, so such a move would make a nonsense out of human rights by bypassing the essence of what it means to be human, namely, the capacity to feel pain. Embodied vulnerability must therefore remain at the centre of human rights based on a clear-cut ethical distinction between corporations and people. The body can be mobilised as a counter-factual to ideas about disembodiment – all rights (not to be tortured/the right to life/shelter and food) focus on the protection of embodied beings, and other rights such as freedom of movement also presuppose a body inhabiting space as an incarnate presence (Grear, 2006).

Once celebrated as cosmopolitanism in action, human rights are now coming under growing, critical scrutiny. The triumphalist age of rights (Bobbio,

2006)[4] has been replaced with scepticism as the vision they embodied has self-evidently unraveled. While rights go back to the French and American Revolutions, it was after 1968 that they came to be idealised as a solution to the violence characteristic of previous utopias such as communism and nationalism, such that social activism navigated eastern and western Europe, as well as the United States and Latin America and promoted the ideal of international law as a peaceful alternative (Moyn, 2012). However, this ideal of human rights unraveled under new political agendas and the euphoria that met the United Nations Declaration of Human Rights (UNDHR) in 1948 now seemed precipitous, which should have been foreseen given that it was not long after the declaration that France, the standard-bearer of human rights, repeatedly violated them in their war against Algerian independence through excessive depravity, including extra-judicial torture and rape (Fanon, 2004 [1961]).

There is no shortage of evidence that the age of human rights was more rhetoric than reality. The break-up of Yugoslavia saw mass graves reminiscent of the World War which had prompted the creation of the UNDHR. Before this, there was the Tiananmen Square massacre, where pro-democracy protesters were killed, detained and executed – their memory recently erased as China has taken steps to retake control of Hong Kong. In Rwanda, a preventable, bloody genocide took place under the gaze of European countries too slow (or unwilling) to stop the chaotic and brutal killing spree. Later, in Egypt, the killing of protesters in the 2008 pro-democracy movement and their detention destroyed the idea of the Middle East becoming the hub of a new, democratic, soft revolution led by the youth. Later again, the genocide of the Rohingya Muslims in Myanmar and the murder of unarmed black Americans by police in the United States all provided convincing testimony to the emptiness of formal, judicial human rights when applied to marginalised, precarious people.

So now theorists are turning their attention to asking how, when human rights had become globally accepted and accredited, such extreme violations remain common and widespread. There is general agreement that it is naïve to view human rights as the ultimate of rights when they have been appropriated most effectively by the rich and powerful at the expense of high ideals of universal justice. The age of rights, it has been claimed, has failed

---

4 It is important to note that Bobbio (2006) was not saying that human rights had triumphed. His argument was more subtle: it was that human rights, democracy and peace were all related and that you could not have one without having them all, and that peace depended on citizenship spreading from the national to the universal.

to disrupt growing inequality but rather co-existed with an uncaring liberal order and hypocritical global governance (Moyn, 2018). The International Criminal Court (ICC) has entrenched rather than assuaged the differential appropriation of human rights by countries from the Global South versus the Global North. To conceptualise the ICC as global in reach and performance is flawed because its cosmopolitanism has, since its inception, been inscribed with the ongoing salience of existing power blocs. The problems with the ICC are most obvious in its encounter with Islam, which explains its limited support from Islamic countries in the Middle East and North Africa (Fouladvand, 2014).

The War on Terror had a formative effect on new social theories on human rights. Agamben (2005) exposed how states of exception led to extreme derogations of human rights by countries recognised as their greatest upholders. Non-citizens in the United States could be held indefinitely on suspicion of being engaged in terrorism. It allowed detainees to be denied legal rights; for Taliban POWs to be deprived of rights and for identity-less people to suffer waterboarding and other acts of torture in Guantanamo Bay and Abu Ghraib – even when the United States holds itself up as the greatest carrier of rights. The removal of legal rights and citizenship of Jews under Nazism is an appropriate comparison. States of emergency, normalised by democratic governments, deprive precarious people of their rights in the pursuit of geopolitical strategies. The War on Terror showed how states of emergency can result in whole populations being cast out of human rights law (Razack, 2008) as in Guantanamo Bay where arbitrarily rounded-up suspects were detained indefinitely without access to lawyers. We cannot necessarily, even as citizens, depend on states for protection because they also have the power to de-nationalise the undesirable, rendering them without state protection and therefore devoid of rights. While not alone in losing her citizenship, Shabina Begum's case has attracted the most attention as an illustration of de-citizenship thought to have been confined to history. A form of banishment and the enactment of a spectacle to ensure that all could see the transformation of a citizen into an enemy. As an example of de-citizenship, Begum's case amounted to 'target practice' for its contemporary use (Stonebridge, 2021).

The scepticism that has replaced triumphalism takes us back to Arendt's (2004 [1949]) contention that human rights amount to nothing if they were not accompanied by membership of a state: this underlay the right to have rights and the stateless were deprived of such rights. While her views were formed by the genocide of the Jews, her theory is a general one and remains salient. Statelessness continues to be widespread today – the Bidoon women in Kuwait, Syrian and Iraqi Kurds, as well as Palestinians in the occupied territories, amongst many others. The Kurdish Rojava movement in Syria has tried to make a merit of this condition – arguing against the fight for a Kurdish state and opting instead for a celebration of statelessness. However, stateless bodies are disposable. Control states, such as Israel, can engage in serious human rights abuses with impunity, normalising the targeted maiming of Palestinians in the occupied territories. Palestinians under Israeli governance are subjected to a slow death based on a security agenda that invokes a normative embodiment through the language of orientalism by presenting Palestinians as backward. This misuse of bodies is how settler colonialism works, where Israel literally makes use of its right to maim, to cripple rather than kill, and debilitate Palestinians living in the occupied territories. A biopolitical governmentality that ensures the obliteration of Palestinian resistance so that maiming is used to strengthen neo-colonialism through a particular brand of state violence (Puar, 2017).

Arguments about globalisation and mobility – hinging on ideas of fluidity and the death of distance – moreover, disguise how the mobility regime also produces new systems of closure and immobility regimes where suspicious people's movements must be contained, providing the basis for the paradigm of suspicion enabled by new technologies (Shamir, 2005). Some people are forced to stay put, so mobility is not just about movement but also immobility – for example, when indigenous communities are dispossessed by others' migration (Ahmed et al., 2003). Vulnerable bodies are often confined and immobilised. Enforced immobility has been the fate of Palestinians in the occupied territory, where Gaza has come to be seen as an open prison. The pain of containment has been captured in the work of artists such as Mona Hatoum, whose artwork, such as *The Negotiating Table*, powerfully exposes the capacity of states for violence in the name of security (Tzelepis, 2016). State violence over bodies is agonisingly clear in the suffering endured by people left to deal with disappearances. Being neither dead nor alive causes untold pain on the families left behind, in a state of suspense with no prospect of closure (Guardiola-Rivera, 2017) in countries such as Colombia and Argentina.

Far from creating more openness and mobility, globalisation has been accompanied by a move towards containment and enclave societies (Turner, 2007). European citizenship's privilege is based on increased bordering that reinforces the disposability of asylum seekers or refugees. There is no new openness to strangers when people show a banal acceptance of bodies swept onto beaches, traced to the continent's history of colonialism, which has led us to question whether a genuine cosmopolitan Europe is possible (Bhambra, 2017). The image of a two-year-old Syrian boy swept onto an Italian beach shook the world, but only briefly, not enough to put an end to the policy of 'No Entry' (Bauman, 1997). Europe's mistreatment – including its failure to provide safe routes, its housing of asylum seekers in unsafe and inhumane detention centres and fast-track processing of alleged illegal migrants – resonates cruelly with past injustices. Bodily hierarchy is etched into our uneven mercy, where Ukrainian refugees are welcomed and African or Middle Eastern ones are not. This hierarchy does not only apply to outsiders; even those who enjoy citizenship rights might have their bodily integrity violated, because it is the nation-state – the home of citizenship – which most often violates rights. Moreover, human rights principles and institutions – underpinned by the principle of bodily commonality – and their main carrier, the nation-state, continue to distinguish between different types of people, with those confined to the bottom of the hierarchy restricted to bare life (Agamben, 2005).

For all these reasons, we need to keep the body at the centre of human rights. However, we must also consider the intimate relationship between the body and dress, which creates other sources of vulnerability. There is a close relationship between the body, dress and identity because it is through dress that we express our identity by signalling our gender, ethnicity, class, religion or culture, and it is through dress that we position ourselves and reveal to others our positionality (Pereira-Aries, 2017). Goffman (1968) demonstrated this when he showed us how stripping people of their clothing removes their sense of self. To strip inmates of their clothing by forcing them to wear institutional clothing is to shed them of their identity. Clothing – its forced removal or surveillance – is one of the many ways a person's identity is either created or erased. This identity can be a collective one, the measure of group identity. The compulsory wearing of the star to mark out Jews in 1930s Germany was an extreme form of degradation and stigma. It affirmed a collective identity while marking out how that identity should be designated for extermination. The hooding of detainees in Guantanamo Bay and Abu Ghraib likewise erased identity with the deliberate purpose of denying them any sense of dignity or identity.

Dress is essential to bodily integrity because it is as human and universal a part of embodiment as the physical body. Performativity through dress is a universal part of being human and signals the importance of transcending the dualism between symbolism and materiality; the notion of performative habitus sheds light on embodiment and bodily dispositions, which are both structured and creative (Goffman, 1968; Butler, 2004). Performativity – albeit through dress – is essential to being human. Dress enables us to express our identity, collective or individual, and is a strong indicator of status, religious identity and other such statuses. It can be used to mobilise cultural capital which can challenge the naïve gaze of others. How we dress as part of our habitus departs, therefore, from the idea of a dressed body as unnatural by recognising that this social process is universal. The habitus is an assemblage of tastes and dispositions that produce actions and practises of individuals and groups towards objects, that is, practises that are not immediately conscious or reflexive. These specificities are accommodated by the more general frame of social groups distinguishing themselves through cultural activities and embodiment (Bourdieu, 1984).

Any theory of human rights must therefore consider how dress is an embodied practise and one that is typically gendered or racialised in public spaces. Given how one's identity is closely aligned with dress, it follows that its regulation by the state counts as a violation of personal embodiment (Entwhistle, 2020). While physical wounding of the body – such as torture – is the hardest of violations, for human rights fully to realise their commitment to bodily integrity they must embrace other universal forms of embodiment, such as dress and clothing. Clothing is already recognised as a human right written into the International Covenant on Economic, Social and Cultural Rights (ICESCR), based on the view that clothing was a fundamental part of life, with some arguing that it was as much a basic human need as food and shelter. This view was endorsed by The Convention on the Rights of the Child (CRC) which called on states to ensure that children not only had the right to basic provisions such as food but also housing and clothing. Despite being centred in the ICESCR, this right has been sidelined and the state's responsibility for enforcing it is limited (Graham, 2022).

However, the ability to perform one's identity through dress, despite its being a universal practise and linked with dignity, does not have a codified human right attached to it, although the closest is the right to manifest one's religion. Yet the body and clothing are so closely related that dress can be understood as a second skin: it both touches the surface of the physical body and looks outward to act as a boundary or frontier. It is this dual aspect of clothing, touching and facing outwards from the body, that connects the physical with the symbolic (Turner, 2012). Human rights' law on clothing ignores the symbolism associated with it. Clothing is a shell but also of the skin as another level of casing. Dress not only protects from the environment but also signals membership of a group and acts as a performative indicator of one's identity. Moreover, it can become contentious when it is thought to transgress the boundary between the private and the public. As such, it is a social and psychological skin and an essential part of how the material body is constructed (Battisti, 2016).

Religious dress is perhaps one of the most powerful and contentious forms of dress in secular and non-secular countries, because most religions use the body as a way of defining who belongs to a particular religion and who does not. The display of hair is a clear case of this – covering is very important – mostly by women under Islam and Judaism and also by men under Sikhism.

The beard is also a critical religious signifier for Muslim men. In secular countries, religious groups use such bodily dispositions and dress (hijabs, turbans) to mark themselves in a way that expresses their religious identity through a self-conscious act of dressing. Thus, it is critical to identity – religious dress and the body are therefore essential to dignity, because religious dress acts to be absorbed as part of the wearer's identity and to be read by others as such (Mahmood, 2001). How the body – the unwanted body – has been subjected to security, management and containment has a long history. Body governance successfully embeds in the public mind the idea of some bodies as unworthy or a threat to the social order, and it is people who wear religious clothing in secular societies who are most likely to be seen as potential transgressors of governmental norms.

The concept of risk management has been used to understand the control of unruly bodies at moments of great upheaval, such as revolutions and warfare, and is central to theories of securitisation which have looked at how governments identify and contain threats through language, law, regulations or institutions dedicated to surveillance. Its emphasis on national governments reflects how, historically, it is nationalist movements that have identified groups of people who should be included or excluded and those who are defined as uncivilised (Guardiola-Rivera, 2010). Nationalism has been responsible for displacing people by removing citizenship, for example (Derrida, 1998) creating dislocation and feelings of not belonging. Said's (1979) theory of orientalism stemmed in part from his personal experience of displacement; he showed how colonial rule in the Middle East had to be rationalised and justified through ideas of Muslimness as both dangerous and exotically infantile. While he did not look specifically at how colonial states secured women's bodies, his work stimulated a wealth of feminist literature on how such processes affected women and how gender and women's bodies were regulated in the Middle East (Abu-Lughod, 2001).

Unveiling Muslim womens' bodies is historically and currently a way of regulating them. In *Algeria Unveiled* (Duara, 2004) Fanon looks at gender's role in nationalist movements, noting how French settlers saw unveiling as a source of liberation but also observing that it was mainly men who supported unveiling and thus suggesting that it partly expressed an idea of the exotic other, pre-empting Said's (1978) critique of the European male gaze. Unveiling was therefore seen as allied with colonial power and explains why Fanon saw Algerian women's freedom as intrinsically linked with national liberation. Women played a part in the fight against French colonialism using their covering to bomb French bars or cafes, using their bodies as a form of resistance. Thus, Fanon saw veiling (in practical or metaphorical terms) as essential to the fight for national liberation (Reid, 2007). While there are many difficulties in Fanon's account of women and covering, the way he essentialised it – it nevertheless says much about the mis(use) of women's dress in national security/conflict contexts.

The question posed here is how virtuous institutions – judicial human rights – may be a part of this project in contemporary times and in those countries – Western liberal democracies – which seek to set themselves apart from other regions in their commitment to equality and diversity and an explicit distancing from any hierarchy of humanity which would lead to some people having less access to rights than others. Such virtuous institutions, moreover, are supra-national, standing above the state to hold it in check and prevent bodily violations – albeit absolute ones or those relating to the intimacy of dress. International Human Rights bodies such as the ICC, ECJ, ECtHR and the UN Human Rights Committee are thought to represent the most virtuous of rights, standing for the rule of law, universalism and cosmopolitanism. Unwanted intrusions into the body, including external control through surveillance, are an affront to the universal use of the body, materially and symbolically. The body is indicative of identity and status, and this is what makes it profoundly human; its precarity can be physical or semiotic. Being deprived of performative embodiment is profoundly damaging to being human, and the universality of the body's performative role means that any transgression is a violation of bodily integrity and identity.

The notion of virtuous institutions is linked to virtue ethics, which enjoyed a revival with the rediscovery of cosmopolitan ethics (Turner, 2002). Human rights – manifest in the growth of global rights institutions – provide an obvious contemporary vehicle for the expression of such an ethic. However, the failure of human rights points to a gap in the consideration of supra-national organisations' role in risk management, including virtuous ones such as global and regional human rights institutions. This book aims to fill this gap, mainly (but not exclusively) in relation to the veiled woman in Europe – the banning of which is a paradigmatic case of disciplining women's bodies. I am not concerned with the many reasons why women might choose to cover or not to cover, but with how human rights, security politics and embodiment come together in an historically controversial manifestation of gendered embodiment, one that not only has religious significance but also cultural and national significance and resistance. The veil has long been a controversial garment, and national governments, albeit those who enforce its wearing (such as Iran) or those who forbid it, are exercising control over women's bodies.

Chapter 2

SECURING UNDESIRABLE BODIES

Biopolitical governance and securitisation affect all religions; however, today's generalised fear of Islam has become a fixation, leading to calls for greater political security involving excessive state bordering and a return to state sovereignty to erase the presumed threat of the Muslim. We have become preoccupied with controlling migration based on a same/other dichotomy framed through the lens of security so that restrictions can be used to stop movement across borders on grounds of dangerous strangers or citizens (Nyers, 2003). The political bordering of bodies has created new technologies of control – such as detention – and strategies of exclusion – such as deportation (Huysmans, 2005). After 9/11, the idea of the perfect suspect – Muslim – created new forms of governance which fuelled a sense of unease about migration as a threat to global security, where profiling technologies to scrutinise, detain or remove unwanted bodies, particularly asylum seekers and so-called illegal refugees – mainly Muslims – were established (Nyers, 2003) and civil liberties and rights were eroded through the mobilisation of elite discourses and institutionalised forms of security (Balzacq, 2016). Popular acceptance of discourses about Muslims as dangerous meant that governments (typically) could push their security agendas through without much protest – the key illustration being the wave of emergency measures that swept across North America and Europe after 9/11 so that clear derogations of human rights were seen as moderate rather than extreme (Bilgin, 2010).

In this context, securitisation theory took the place of human security by overturning the emphasis on policies to protect people from poverty or terrorism, with a perspective that highlighted the negative aspects of security agendas and politics, shedding light on their potentially harmful ramifications and the creation of new, existential insecurities. Ideas about discipline, biopolitics and technologies of security fitted seamlessly into its framework and showed how colonialism, its sediments and residues, continued to be carried into metropolitan centres to contribute to the subjugation of people deemed backward and dangerous. It has shown how security agendas created and sustained through language have joined up with technological and administrative practises such as border control policies involving a dedicated band of professional security personnel. Securitisation through speech has coalesced with practises such as profiling, risk assessment and the rise of security professionals, fusing to ensure successful securitisation (Bigo, 2010). Examples such as Frontex and other private groups exposed how states deployed non-state actors to pursue their security agendas, so there was a decentralisation of securitising measures and forms of governance that sustained social order in the public sphere through state coercion alongside non-state allies (Butler, 2020). Undesirable bodies became vulnerable to new forms of violence like biometric techniques that acted as identity management by states that construct mythical threats, the most obvious being undeserving asylum seekers whose biometric management has significant implications for citizenship based on a 'dispositif of security' (Muller, 2004). The immaterial forms of state power such as virtual and biometric borders mean that borders are becoming quasi-permanent states of exception, targeting mainly migrants (Duran, 2010) but also minority cultures expressed through the body, including Muslim dress.

The recent obsession and securitisation of the Muslim woman's dress can partly be understood through the so-called visual turn in securitisation theory. Denmark's use of the Mohammed cartoon controversy to convey an immediate sense of threat and danger to justify increased security is an example of this. Securitising moves based on visuality are effective because the visual image is easy to circulate, and it has an immediacy that demands an instant, emotive response based on the image of an enemy. Images have a communicative function and spectacular ones in real time such as the coverage of the falling towers and jumping people on 11 September, the photos from Abu Ghraib and the Muhammed Cartoon Crisis are especially powerful. The issue is that what are immediately simple images become the force for intervention and action – as the Cartoon Crisis shows, whose fallout included demonising cartoon versions of Mohammed and intelligence service activity (Hansen, 2011). The image of the veiled woman carries the potential for visual securitisation. She is inscrutable and therefore deemed to be unavailable to the usual security practises – hence her illegalisation by several Western liberal democracies. In contrast, the image of the hijabi fashionista is innocent and unthreatening because it sits comfortably with our ideas of what free women should look like: even if they wear the hijab, they adhere to our consumerist values around fashion. The securitising potential of visual images was powerfully demonstrated through *Time*'s image of Aisha – shot by the Taliban – and defiantly standing up against them. A good, covered, Muslim woman presented as unthreatening to security (Heck and Schlag, 2013).

Security politics and securitisation are (ideally at least) at odds with human rights because these rights are supposed to protect vulnerable people who have been subjected to excessive security processes and whose movement has been curtailed despite having genuine reasons for moving and where surveillance methods have led to their containment (Bigo, 2017). Bodies that move from poorer countries to richer ones are portrayed as illegal and a risk to the places they are going to, so those of us who live in the rich world see ourselves as in a perpetual state of war against supposed invaders, which plays on ideas of immaterial borders replacing territorial ones (Balibar, 2010). This negative circle is especially salient in extreme measures of securitisation, for example when children (separated from their parents) were held in cages under the Trump regime, along with calls for new walls to be built. It is within this framework of heightened bodily regulation that we can understand the United Kingdom's plan announced in 2022 to deport asylum seekers crossing the English Channel from France to Rwanda – an authoritarian country with a poor human rights record – for assessment of their claims and, if successful, to be granted refugee status in Rwanda. Human rights charities denounced the scheme as chilling and immoral. While the UK government paraded itself as a country that welcomes refugees, this new policy exposed how unconvincing this projected image was. It presented its move as a method to deter people trafficking – founded on baseless humanitarian principles: safe, legal passage was an obvious and better deterrent. The policy was announced when the government was trying (half-heartedly) to enable refugees from Ukraine to settle in the United Kingdom. The stark juxtaposition of two kinds of asylum seekers and refugees – white, Christian Ukrainians (welcomed, sort of) and darker-skinned people from Syria, Africa and other conflict zones (unwelcomed) – uncovered how some people are more valued than others and the notion of unequal mercy.

Much of this work has centred on the state's securitising role. The securitising role of benign, supra-national virtuous institutions including human rights ones – such as the European Court of Human Rights (ECtHR) or the ICC – has been absent. Because they are supposed, by default, to be exempt from such closure practises and instead committed to openness towards strangers and empathy for distant others or those who are not like us (Boltanski, 1999). Human rights were supposed to signify a move towards a post-national light in the time of globalisation where they, along with cosmopolitanism, were presented as the means for figuring the global as human and placing actual and ideal constraints on national culture and sovereignty (Cheah, 2006). This was their promise. The promise has meant that the less benign practises of global human rights have been missing from securitisation theory. Its state-centric limitation has partially been remedied by looking at non-state actors – including multinational corporations, policy think tanks, inter-governmental organisations, as well as local militia groups – and this has raised two connected questions, namely, how non-state actors may adopt a security role and how they have undercut the state's role. However, virtuous supra-national institutions, their security role and their relationship with other non-state actors and the state in executing security acts, have not been considered. This is particularly important given how the new security environment now operates in a multi-level way: national, local, regional and global levels, undermining the claim that the state has a monopoly over violence (Butler and Wolf in Butler, 2020).

Virtuous supra-national human rights institutions are an especially interesting case study because their very existence is to act as a check on disproportionate state securitisation of vulnerable groups and to prevent such bodies from the indignity of excessive bodily intrusion, to act as an audience and neutral arbiter of excessive state control. The limited attention on how virtuous transnational institutions might be complicit in security agendas is therefore a significant gap, and this leads us to the question of, if so, how. Is it possible that supra-national virtuous institutions such as the ICC, ECJ and ECtHR might also become agents of security politics and either fail to prevent bodily wounding or contribute to it themselves? If so, how do they become embroiled in security acts and abandon the role of neutral audience and arbiter of security politics?

Human rights' implication in securitising racialised and gendered bodies is significant because women and minorities comprise groups whose access to such rights has been limited because of their disproportionate subjection to security politics (Ibrahim, 2005; Bilgin, 2010, 2011). Human rights have never been that virtuous given their exclusionary origins and even in the post-war euphoric phase their commitment to the white, propertied man rather than vulnerable groups such as women, the non-propertied, refugees and minorities who remained outside of them (Stonebridge, 2021). Moreover, with its emphasis on discursive aspects of securitisation, it is vital to recognise those who are silenced and their vulnerabilities: it is often the most vulnerable who face the most danger when they break their silence. This is relevant because it explains how national, religious and racial groups might turn to other forms of bodily agency to protest, demonstrating the need to sustain a focus on the body and its security or insecurity depending on the way it is viewed and whose precarity can be affected by discourses that do not recognise their insecurity. There is, therefore, a need for a critical analysis of how gender and (in)security – in some cases, race and racialised insecurity – has been produced (Hansen, 2020).

We therefore need to look at how securitisation applies to the vulnerable, silenced or immobilised body because it is on such bodies that security practises loop back to human rights and precarity and insecurity. New security technologies have enabled vigilance of what is inside the clothed body. This is one of the implications for citizenship resulting from a post-9/11 obsession with international security. Biometric technologies result in a management of identity and, in this respect the invasion of the public body is a direct challenge to citizenship by transforming ideas of agency, in relation to vulnerable groups such as asylum seekers whose citizenship rights are restricted through these processes, which amounts to securitisation from the inside and can enable the disqualification of some bodies from citizenship (Muller, 2004). New technologies have intensified the surveillance of bodies through, in one obvious case, the use of scanners in border control. These scanners are designed to go beneath our clothing and to reveal our unclothed bodies. They amount to a virtual strip search that invades personal privacy in the name of disproportionate ideas about risk, where everyone is identified as a possible threat. This practice involves rendering transparency and visibility with security (Amir and Kotef, 2018). Ultimately, such new biometrics, by enabling the disqualification of certain bodies from citizenship rights, means that we might be left with the question of what is left of citizenship (Muller, 2004). But this trend, which undermines access to citizenship rights, also has profound implications for human rights – the core of which remains the body.

The question of audience in securitisation theory needs more attention: Who is the audience of securitising measures? Who is listening? And who, as audience, either buys or dispels ideas about threats? The concept of audience is a central part of this theory because of its emphasis on securitisation as an inter-subjective process: the success of a securitising act depends on whether it is accepted or not by an audience. This raises the question of what audience securitisation theory is thinking about: and often, it is the public. It is the intersection between those who practise security and those who observe it that is critical to whether a securitising move is successful. It is only when a security threat enjoys the support of an audience – the public, for example – that it becomes effective and embedded, and why the focus on intersubjectivity is a key to securitisation theory (Balzacq, 2005; Stritzel, 2007).

We therefore need to look more closely at the audience of security politics and the politics of acceptance and complicity. Securitising measures take place that enable the audience to engage in such moves, which might include elites, the populace, technocratic or scientific organisations. The assumption of an ongoing iterative process between speaker and audience leads us to ask how rather than did a securitising move take place. While Salter's (2008) fourfold schema of potential audiences is interesting, it remains statist by its attention on state actors who identify an existential threat that requires emergency executive powers and, if successful, depoliticise by embedding a security issue outside the rules of normal politics. It is not enough to conceptualise the audience as one that accepts exceptional procedures or has been convinced by the arguments presented to it because this is simply an assumption. There may, for example, be competing audiences subjected to speech acts who will interpret them in very different ways, impacting on outcomes. The context of those listening to presentations of a security threat is critical because it positions them in differential relations to the speech act and decisions about whether to authorise an action. The audience is not a passive receptor of security messages but an agentic component of its inter-subjective nature, and there is a need to identify the audience and investigate its role in the securitisation process (Côté, 2016). We need therefore to consider supranational virtuous institutions such as human rights ones that have the power to hold national governments to account and are assumed to be exempt from compliance with security agendas and therefore presumed to be a neutral audience. Supra-national human rights institutions constitute a particularly compelling example of the audience. Their role is actively to observe, monitor and check the excessive use of power and to protect vulnerable people. They are supposed to be neutral and detached from state politics.

Human rights' ability to challenge governmental discourses is contingent, and there is evidence that governmental elites might mobilise human rights as part of a securitising move, sometimes informed by religious nationalism (Nunez-Mietz, 2019). Human rights might comply with securitising politics and become accomplices in the disempowerment of citizens because they have fallen into the trap of surveillance realism, that is a pragmatic acceptance that precludes active attempts to hold securitising powers to account (Dencik and Cable, 2017). For this reason, the two social groups that need special protection from human rights – vulnerable communities and activists fighting for the right to have rights – may be victims of human rights' banal engagement in security politics, leading these groups to be the most securitised of all without access to rights protections (Krasteva, 2017). Human rights, in secular Europe, have been mobilised by political leaders and parties as well as populist feminism to prevent the rights of covered women. Judicial human rights, where claims have been taken to supra-national courts, have been an audience to this, authorised with the power to curtail such governmental misuse of human rights.

Security and insecurity are related as practises of security, superficially in place to offer protection and stability, can have the opposite effect and generate insecurity rather than security. Moreover, state-level insecurity is critical to the production of disproportionate securitisation. A vicious circle begins where security causes insecurity, which in turn promotes a greater perceived need for security, which reinforces security politics to the extent that they become normalised through various processes of political exclusion, of surveillance, of data collection, of encampment, profiling and registration. First-level securitisation relates principally to external borders and exclusion by producing a discourse that constructs migrants and refugees as a source of terrorism and crime, and second-level securitisation focusses on alleged chronic threats and attends to internal boundaries and exclusion, including exclusion from taken-for-granted citizenship rights. These two levels interact in a way that creates security talk about violence such as terrorism and crime and threats to economic stability, welfare provision and national identity – especially those minorities who do not assimilate (Banal and Kreide, 2017). Here, we are concerned with second-level security and how challenges to these measures need to mobilise human rights for political reasons, highlighting their failings, to progress towards a common good (Kreide, 2015).

There is no more an ideal audience, in the context of post-democracy, than global human rights organisations. These should be the ultimate arbiter: the truth-tellers and the route to which vulnerable, over-scrutinised bodies should be able to turn to for protection of their rights. Yet the concept of audience has not been applied to institutions that are held to high standing, holding values that should compel them to act as a check on disproportionate security politics at the national level that targets vulnerable groups, which means this notion needs further analysis (Williams, 2011). Doing so in relation to virtuous institutions is particularly interesting because it tests assumptions about their supposed benign character. Human rights are assumed to have a (de-) securitising role in political conflicts that target vulnerable people. Human rights NGOs might be well-placed to lobby against state portrayals of enemies, including enemies within, and seek to prevent such views from becoming popularly embedded. However, to what extent do judicial human rights, made up of elites who relate to governmental elites, challenge disproportionate measures against those deemed unfit, and under what circumstances are they likely not to act as de-securitising agents? (Georgi, 2016).

Because human rights are typically enforced by nation-states, supranational bodies, whose role is to rein in national power, may not act as ultimate arbiters but rather defer to national political impulses and trends. Migrants should in principle be entitled to the human rights that are contained in the major Conventions such as the ICCPR and the ICESCR, yet we see the states signing up to these treaties refusing entry to refugees and international human rights law failing to halt this growing trend. The subservience to national bodies by human rights is clear in how, even though citizens and non-citizens can take cases to the court, any abuse can only be resolved through a change in national legislation. The European Convention of Human Rights might oversee its signatories, but the dualistic nature of the system enables European law to be interpreted domestically (Nash, 2009) and therefore an unreliable arbiter or audience to protect vulnerable people from national abuses. Human rights as securitising instruments have been exposed in the case of migration in Europe and, as one example, in the case of the Roma, who are regarded as not proper rights bearers and thus cast out of human rights protections. So, how human rights confront a security threat is not a given if the alleged threat is not seen as a desirable body. They have been seen wanting in the face of contemporary bordering because they remain committed to the notion of an ideal political community, so they fail to prevent No Entry policies and might well reinforce modern borders' role in practises of securitisation, both without and within Europe and act as a mode of governance of European citizens, especially the vulnerable ones, as refugees have come to be seen as a permanent threat to the public order. Human rights have, in relation to migration and unpopular minorities, exercised a power to securitise (Kreide in Van Baar, 2019).

Chapter 3

VIRTUOUS INSTITUTIONS AND THE SECURITISATION OF WOMEN'S BODIES

As we have seen, the securitisation of unwanted, vulnerable and precarious bodies often takes place in public spaces, and we have looked at some of the hardest cases of this, such as Israel's intentional policy to maim Palestinians (Puar, 2017), or depriving asylum seekers and refugees of their rights through bordering measures that increase insecurity for those refused safe passage, held in detention centres, subjected to extreme forms of surveillance and threats of deportation after arrival. Increasingly restrictive policies aim to deter asylum seekers through multiple means so that arrival at a safe third country becomes meaningless when those who succeed are likely to face detention, minimal welfare benefits and family reunification rights. Such poor treatment and the erosion of the most minimal of welfare indicate that international human rights' guarantee of basic rights has become vacuous (Edwards, 2005) such that both hard and soft rights have been lost.

While there is an understandable focus on violations such as torture, bodily integrity through dress should also be considered. The regulation of religious dress, especially women's, in Europe has become a significant focus. It is not just refugees that are subjected to securitisation, but also unpopular minority citizens – whose citizenship should protect them. In today's Europe, Muslims are considered the most dangerous minority, and this chapter explores how human rights institutions have failed to protect the bodily integrity of European Muslims at the point when Muslim citizens – historically excluded from shaping the public sphere – have started to demand their place in it and to be treated as European citizens (Jonker and Amiraux, 2015). The enablement of religious pluralism – through religious dress – in secular public spaces tests human rights' commitment to bodily integrity in circumstances where demands for recognition clash with a national security climate. Thus far, European case law seems to be lagging the vision that supra-national judicial rights are a neutral arbiter, audience and an effective check on national governments who regard overt expressions of Muslim identity – in particular, the covered Muslim woman – as a threat to the normal order of things. The public sphere is essential to the enactment of human rights as a way of transgressing exclusionary national culture where those deemed not to belong are unwelcome. This chapter is about how rights talk and law can be complicit in securitising vulnerable groups.

Despite there being no evidence that the covered Muslim woman is a national security threat, she has become an obsession for many European governments (Baldi, 2018) because she is a contentious body and so a legitimate target for governmental security politics.[1] Now, covered Muslim women in Europe have become the suspect community where the control of terrorism has turned to Muslim dress (Bigo, 2016). Her new, public, bodily dispositions signal a commitment to Islam that is especially controversial in Europe, but novel and visible displays of Islam in Muslim-majority countries have also disrupted previously homogeneous and uncontroversial public spaces. All over the world, Muslims are engaging in new ways of being in public – which might be religious or secular – but which, often, have a bodily aspect whose new visibility is seen as threatening (Göle, 2002). One of the most recent illustrations is the wave of protests in Iran, where, by pulling off their coverings, women have engaged in calls for the end of the regime sparked off by the death of a Kurdish woman who was beaten by the morality police for not wearing a headscarf.[2]

The rise in covering in secular public spaces are rebellious acts of citizenship (Isin, 2008) and, unused to such visible acts, governments see these as threatening because they depart from the safety of past generations' assimilationism. Most challenging is that women who veil in public now are more middle class, mobile and integrated than their mothers; they speak the language of their countries and believe they have a right to assert their identity. Casting their backgrounds aside, young Muslim women are challenging the popular view of them as passive victims of oppression by a misogynistic culture. They are adopting new forms of visibility which disrupt the secular public sphere, and this rebellion is about freedom from being confined to the margins in favour of moving into the centre of social life, actively saying no to oppression and yes to the free expression of their religious identity (Göle, 2011).

---

1 This is an unfounded response because Muslim women have generally not been involved in terrorist incidents, and only a tiny minority chooses to wear full covering.

2 https://www.theguardian.com/world/2022/oct/04/iranian-schoolgirls-take-up-battlecry-as-protests-continue

Governments across Europe are unnerved by this sizeable generation of Muslims (women and men) signalling that they are not afraid to come out of the shadows into public spaces displaying their religious commitment. This development centres on four main practises: wearing a veil or a beard (men); claiming the right to prayer sites and to halal food, all seen as acts of defiance and presented as threats to the social order. However, veiling has become a particular fixation because it undermines the prevailing view that covering signifies subordination where sexual inequalities in the West have been covered up (Balibar, 2007). Wearing the veil upends ideas about agency through bodily disposition and instead signals collective empowerment by defying checks in the public sphere. This is a process of reversal which compels us to reflect on how so-called traditional practises might act as a creative route to reversing negative meanings into positive ones.

Visibility in the public sphere is an active display of citizenship: wearing the veil reverses the stigma attached to it and defiantly challenges age-old stereotypes about Islamic backwardness (Gole, 2017). While this drive is a positive one in freeing open identification with Islam from the private to the public, the environment of mistrust has not only turned this new generation of Muslims into distrustful citizens for governments but also for the majority. While being a personal intimate garment (Mahmood, 2011) the veil has come to be seen as a symbol of resistance and transgression. The tiny numbers of women who wear full covering in France created a huge public and political reaction, with the veil being described as ostentatious by the French government seeking to ban it. Successive governments across Europe began to portray veiling as acts of defiance in the public space, glossing over the many reasons a woman might cover, preferring to regard it as proselytising or an act of submission.

As we have seen, Europe's Muslims have been subjected to securitisation around four main areas, each mobilising old ideas about backward and unclean practises. Covering has been the most controversial, accompanied by praying in public and mosque construction; halal food (ritual slaughter) and reverence of sacred figures such as the Prophet. The debates around these practises are regionally differentiated: some global, some pan-European and others more local. Veiling was portrayed as a breach of women's rights; Halal a breach of animal rights; building mosques, minarets and praying an affront to secularism; and circumcision a form of bodily harm. The backlash transcended the usual borders of Europe, where countries such as Denmark joined others through the cartoon controversy and various affairs created new prohibitions. So, the headscarf affair became the veiling debate, which became the burka issue, and then the burkini, leading to a false familiarisation such that non-Muslims thought they knew what these words meant.

Policing of these acts often are not framed in religious terms, so for example, the burkini in the Côte d'Azur was presented as unhygienic and anti-feminist (Göle, 2017).

Muslim women propelling religious identity into the centre of metropolitan Europe, rejecting their peripheral location for one at the centre of public life in major cities, was all the more unsettling for the authorities because it was middle-class Muslims rather than ghettoised ones who were behind these visible acts, engaging in colonial blowback (Balibar, 2007). Such acts of reversal took European governments back to times when religious visibility was an active form of resistance by colonised subjects, talking back to their oppressors and refusing to accept oppression (Owens, 2017). European national governments are facing Muslim women demanding to be visible European citizens who can display their religious and cultural difference in public, which has led to women's bodies being implicated in the confrontation between essentialised conceptions of religion and culture and state power, albeit liberal democratic with a stated commitment to multiculturalism accompanying globalisation's reversal (Benhabib, 2004).

Veiling, as a form of corporeal defiance and a site of resistance, has led to multiple legal bans. Echoing the past, where women were forcibly unveiled by colonial powers, covering has long been seen as the antithesis of modernity and a retreat to the past and to a religion – Islam. The alleged historical threat has been seamlessly transmuted into a new threat to national security, regarded as a political badge signifying risk rather than a benign religious commitment (Göle, 2002). Muslim women who choose to cover are interesting because their voluntary adoption of stigma takes courage, and this explains why it is deemed to be deliberately provocative. The adoption of stigmatised dress forces it to become a visible and an intrusive form of embodiment, transcending the private/public sphere just as praying in public or wearing a beard do (Göle, 2003).

This historical symbolism and legacy forced a minor public phenomenon into national crises, triggering the rapid spread of securitising Muslim women's bodies through Europe. That such a minority practise was considered so dangerous meant that excessive regulatory measures turned into calls for bans of various forms of coverings, crossing borders at an ever-growing rate within the EU. Many European countries enacted outright bans on full-face covering in public spaces, a trend that began in France, swiftly followed by Belgium, before spreading to include countries as diverse as Germany, the Netherlands, Italy, Spain, Switzerland and Denmark. While the ban on the burkini in 2016 was overturned by France's highest administrative court, several cities along the French Riviera continued it. France has instituted national bans; Spain, Switzerland and Germany have allowed individual municipalities to decide on whether to implement bans or not. Several towns in Italy have local bans on face-covering, and some mayors from the anti-immigrant Northern League also banned the use of Islamic swimsuits. In Germany, half of its 16 states banned teachers from wearing headscarves. In Spain, Barcelona announced a ban on full Islamic face-veils in some public spaces, such as municipal offices, public markets and libraries.[3] In Germany, Angela Merkel opposed the burka for preventing integration, and Denmark recently (August 2018) began its policing of the full-face veil in Copenhagen.[4]

Governmental elites mobilised human rights as a securitising tool to repeatedly justify the disproportionate management of Muslim women's bodies and, in doing so, propagate a civilisationist ideology. Elite discourses openly stated that covered women needed to be educated into higher standards of civilisation to count as properly European. The state, by banning these new forms of embodiment, effectively disqualified this minority of women from full and equal membership of the European public sphere. Governments portrayed the covered woman as a serious security problem to justify differential treatment, regulation and containment despite having no supporting evidence. Essentially, the veiled woman was a woman who had made the wrong choice, justifying rescue narratives to protect these women from an oppressive, misogynistic culture in the name of 'progressive' values, colliding old orientalist and colonialist rhetoric with new popular nationalism (Sabsay, 2012). National leaders spoke nostalgically about Enlightenment principles – particularly freedom and dignity for women. In France, which led the wave of bans, Presidents Sarkozy, Hollande and Macron defended excluding covered women from public spaces on the grounds of women's rights to freedom and equality. Macron problematised the veil as oppressive, seeking to persuade women to uncover for self-protection and arguing that France needs to convince covered women that the headscarf or burka does not 'conform to the civilities of French society' and contrasts unambiguously with France's efforts to promote women's rights and gender equality, whose importance needs to be explained.[5]

This led to extraordinary legislation controlling how women should dress: whether they should be covered – and told to uncover – or be uncovered and told to cover, lest they invite sexual assault. Not just governmental elites engaged in this; the judiciary too. Deciding when/if and how women should

3 www.bbc.co.uk/news/world-europe-13038095.
4 https://www.bbc.co.uk/news/world-europe-45064237.
5 https://www.express.co.uk/news/world/946947/emmanuel-macron-muslim-women
-islam-burqa-headscarf-ban-france.

cover or expose their bodies is based on normative positions of how women should present themselves in public. Judicial human rights have taken an arbitrary rather than consistent approach to this question, ranging from interfering with others' legal rights, to oppression if covered, to being unable to teach or have meaningful interaction if covered, to the maintenance of harmony. Contrarily, when judging women for wearing too little, reasons have ranged from dressing in a way that makes them seem permissive and so implicating themselves in the event of assault, to appearing like sex-workers and not acting properly. Juxtaposing these two judgements exposes how paradoxical legal and public views on women's dress are (Beaman, 2013).

These moves against Muslim embodiment in public spaces are part of an imaginary New Europe (Amiraux, 2013) though legalised control over women's bodies, a movement that is not confined to Europe but is transnational, spreading across Europe and across the Atlantic to Canada. The new embodied visibility of Muslims in the European Union triggered transnational controversies that challenged notions of citizenship that continue to rest on mistrust and accommodate nationally sanctioned forms at the expense of forms of diversity to the extent that Muslims have been left unprotected by the law and are cast out of European polities (Amiraux, 2016). Although the United States has distinguished itself by accepting covering in public based on its constitutional commitment to religious expression, women who covered faced a spike in hate crimes, in part ignited by Donald Trump's campaign to 'Make America Great Again' (Welborne et al., 2018).

Our entry into a period of unbound security creates enemies and fears, mainly about a supposed alien presence and has had particularly regulating implications for covered women. Mobilising around securitisation is not a reaction to real threats but does create ideas about dangerous spaces and practises, which makes not only the target of security politics insecure and uneasy but the wider population too (Huysmans, 2014). Securitisation practices depend upon the production of enemies, even when imagined, to generate a sense of relentless insecurity by using techniques of control and processes of normalisation of a threat that lead to a sense of non-belonging amongst those designated the enemy, developments that particularly affect unpopular nomadic communities (Kreide, 2019). Muslims perfectly fit these criteria, being members of a diasporic community united by a commitment to a global ummah and resistance.

Such widespread ideas have created dramas about groups considered to be special threats, and they are typically an already stigmatised group. In the popular imagination, the terrorist look-alike might be the bearded Middle Eastern man (Puar, 2017) or a Middle Eastern man who wears a backpack in the underground, with such conceptions leading to tragedies such as that of

Charles de Menezes. Now it is the covered Muslim women in Europe who are portrayed as a danger, not just to security but to our way of living and cultural values. The covered woman is deemed a source of fear because she defies the technologies of surveillance just as she defies the gaze of others. She is depicted as hard to subject to surveillance regimes. She invokes memories of Europe's colonialist struggles, including the Algerian War of Independence, where liberation fighters used the veil as a disguise and where French colonialists forcibly unveiled Algerian women. The covered woman came to symbolise resistance to Western domination.

With the rise of multiculturalism and the religious pluralism associated with it, governments in pluralistic societies seek to manage their religious minorities by adopting strategies of integration and assimilation, which are used to domesticate minority groups (Turner, 2011). The human rights narrative mobilised by government elites protects only those Muslim women who are seen to belong, namely those who do not cover and assimilate into the mainstream community. Such assimilationist methods are disguised as progressive by emphasising reintegration, liberty and freedom for women (Huysmans, 2005). The discourse of human rights for minorities in Europe changed into one of security, where they were depicted as a threat to the very social fabric of Europe. So, for the very small minority of women who choose to cover, they can only exercise their human rights by electing to uncover.

Counter-mobilisations against the bans have turned the language of human rights against those who see themselves as their standard-bearers. Covered women's protests insisted on the right to be both French and Muslim, displayed by wearing the colours of the tricolour on headscarves. This form of jurisgenerative politics advocates the rights of others and has the potential to produce political transformation through debates in the public sphere between various actors such as Muslim women, Imams, the government, media and human rights organisations. In making such rights claims, these women rejected a passive, docile persona in favour of an active subjectivity based on an assertion of citizenship rights and national belonging (Benhabib, 2004). In holding up the mirror in this way, these individuals and groups are appropriating rights-based discourses as part of a new, active citizenship where the authority of the governing institutions is challenged (Barras, 2009) in a way the governing classes would have most difficulty objecting to.

One would think that European jurisprudence developed by the ECtHR would act as a check on national governments' discriminatory regulation of women's dress given that its protocols include the freedom of thought, conscience and religion with the general protection of rights without discrimination based on religion and for member states to respect religious convictions (Rorive, 2008). On this premise, Muslim women engaged in strategic litigation to win the right to religious expression in public have been unsuccessful, despite rights'-based activism offered formal human rights' institutions the opportunity to transcend the gap between diversity and universalism and allow Muslim women to exercise their freedom of religious expression as national citizens (Brown, 2012).

However, thus far every case has seen the ECtHR fail to protect bodily integrity. Time and again watershed cases such as *Sahin v. Turkey*, *Dahlab v. Switzerland*, *Dogru v. France*, *Kervanci v. France* and *Ludin v. Germany*, which revolved around bans on the hijab in schools, universities and workplaces, failed with judgements acquiescing with governmental defences that the headscarf symbolised male oppression of women and a risk to public order. National bans on wearing the burka in public led to the notable cases of *SAS v. France*, *Dakir v. Belgium* and *Samia Bekcacemi* and *Yamina Oussar v. Belgium*. Despite the complainants testifying that they had been free to choose to cover, their testimony was overridden (Amiraux, 2013). The Court's decision-making used stereotypes of Muslim women, simultaneously portraying them as women needing to be rescued from violent men and women who aggressively propagate their views without any evidence to support their judgements (Rorive, 2008). The complainants' submissions showed that they were not acting under pressure but with agency, alleging that their human rights had been violated in relation to various articles in the Convention, including the right to religious expression and for such freedom to be enjoyed without discrimination against religious minorities or other statuses and appealing to the principle of pluralism.

In accepting the governments' defence that full covering prevented positive interaction between people, jeopardising the possibility of 'living together' (*vivre ensemble*) and fell short of the 'minimum requirement of civility that is necessary for social interaction', the ECtHR manifestly committed itself to a civilisationist and securitising position. This exposed how the ECtHR accepted the French and Belgian defences based on the appropriation of a concept originally embodied in the French Constitutional Court's judgement which implied that individualisation, and thus even democracy itself, was threatened by face covering (Burchardt et al., 2019). The ECtHR's assimilationist and secularising stance meant that its decision-making was more allied with the retreat of multiculturalism than the protection of minority rights and religious freedoms. The Court's use of a dubious legal concept to deny covered women their right to religious expression by claiming that the obstacle to the realisation of human rights was the Muslim woman's refusal to comply with European standards of what it means to be able to communicate harmoniously, endorsing old orientalist thinking. This view reflects a secularist rhetoric that posits the Western modern invention of face-to-face interaction as a universal signification of civilisation (Fournier, 2013).

The Court justified its decision-making on the grounds that there was no domestic consensus within Europe, expressing its attachment to subsidiarity. In so doing, it abandoned its role as a check on state power by failing to establish an overarching consensus on such a politically sensitive ban. Instead, in *Belcacemi and Oussar v. Belgium*, for example, the Court held that the principle of subsidiarity should be prioritised and the question of protection of others should be left to domestic governments. Complicity with governmental securitisation was instrumentalised by an inappropriately high level of commitment to the subsidiarity of the Convention. It should not have been beyond the ECtHR to have found some evidential basis for its judgement that wearing the veil could disrupt public order and infringe the dignity of others. By ignoring contrary evidence, the Court unthinkingly endorsed the security narrative that disproportionately targeted a soft target: the Muslim veil. While *Lachri v. Belgium* was an exception to this blanket ban, it was on the grounds that Ms Lachri was a civil party in a criminal case and not a representative of any public office (Edmunds, 2021).

Far from being a neutral arbiter and an audience whose role is to act as a check on excessive securitisation processes, the Court's conception of itself as adhering to neutrality and impartiality in relation to national states in their assessment of the legitimacy of religious beliefs and/or their expression was meaningless (Rorive, 2008). The Court's decision-making clearly showed no independent thinking, merely a knee-jerk adoption of governmental national security agendas which prohibited covering on implausible grounds – necessary misogyny; a propensity to proselytise extremism – without any evidential basis. The burka cases introduced a new defence, namely that covering prevented positive interaction between people, jeopardising the possibility of living together *(vivre ensemble)*. The judgements thus failed to protect Muslim women from national violations of their rights and relied on a vague and non-legal concept based on a constructed ideal of what counts as harmonious interaction (Steinbach, 2015). The ideal of living together was not legally valid, and there was no evidence of jeopardising public order to the extent that the Court agreed with the unfounded, notion that face covering threatened democracy itself (Burchardt et al., 2019).

Mirroring the national bans, the Court argued that their upholding was compatible with human rights and assumed that Muslim women were resisting European ideals of harmonious communication. Such an assumption reflects a secularist rhetoric that posits the Western modern invention of face-to-face interaction as a universal signification of civilisation, excluding those who do not conform (Fournier, 2013). The stress on living together could have been rendered compatible with the pluralism and tolerance potentially inscribed in the cases. However, it was Muslims and not the majority who had to compromise over what living together means. Tolerating religious symbols in the public sphere rather than banning them would signify a more open and pluralistic society, and moreover, the judgements were not based on evidence (Ati, 2019).

By unreflectingly adopting ideas about the transgressive nature of the veil, the ECtHR, this most virtuous of institutions, became a vehicle of securitisation by hijacking governmental security agendas and deeming full covering to be a threat to public order. In all the cases that the ECtHR has adjudicated on to date involving women wearing the hijab or the burka, it has deferred to the national governments' security agenda, abandoning its role as a neutral audience and a check on excessive state power in favour of complying with state narratives about the threat posed to public order by the wearing of a simple garment by a tiny minority of European Muslim women. In so doing, it has reinforced the view that European Muslims are a threat to national security rooted in a long-held picture of national minorities as disloyal and irredentist (Banting and Kymlicka, 2006) and undermined the human rights of citizens in a gendered and racialised way (Brown, 2020). Acceptance of governmental arguments in favour of the ban shows how the Court has sanctioned the state's increasing intrusion into people's private lives and appropriated its securitising role (Baldi, 2018).

Its judgements enabled state surveillance and disciplinary tactics exercised on the bodies of national citizens considered resistant to modernist ideology (Motha, 2007) and condoned the view that women who cover their faces are not free agents, but passive subjects reinforced by state governance of women's bodies (Behiery, 2013). Judicial human rights have, rather than protect the Muslim woman's body, sanctioned the idea that covering could possibly disrupt social cohesion. France has, of course, been at the centre of this tension because of its tradition of *laïcité* which has been challenged by public performance of religious identity by religious minorities, particularly Muslims, resulting in the *de facto* limit to the right to individual freedom of conscience (Amiraux, 2016). The Court, instead of challenging national governmental bans, claimed that the national state was free to limit religious expression, for example, wearing the headscarf, if the exercise of that freedom clashes with the aim of protecting the rights and freedoms of others, public order and public safety (Rorive, 2008).

The ECtHR's compliance with state defences thus betrayed its core function of protecting human embodiment based on a universal shared bodily vulnerability which underpins cultural differences: shared bodily frailty when their fundamental role is to defend people from bodily denigration, which might include persecution, incarceration, discrimination and exclusion and also dress, which, as we have seen, is about gendered embodiment

(Entwhistle, 2020). The ECtHR judgements buttressed rather than reduced the Muslim woman's precariousness by forcing women to unveil and erasing central public aspects of Muslim identity (Leckey, 2013). The legal judgements endorsed particularly disturbing cases such as when a woman was forced to remove her burkini on a beach with armed police officers standing over her (Baldi, 2016) which is a legally sanctioned form of gender-based violence, denigrating and humiliating women by stripping them of clothing. The Nice incident is an especially ugly case because the woman involved was forced to remove clothing in a public space, representing the opposite of supposedly freeing a Muslim woman from the misogyny of her culture. Such violence was enabled by a state apparatus which successfully depicted the body of the Muslim woman as a symbol of terror, who threatened the existence of the liberal, secular state (Brayson, 2019).

Moreover, the case outcomes were at odds with human rights' NGOs such as Amnesty International or Human Rights Watch and demonstrated how their judicial versions can be turned against the most vulnerable of bodies (Kreide, 2019). Forcible undressing is justified by a discourse which suggests that women's freedom and gender equality is ensured by the uncovering of women's bodies and releases them from the tyranny of traditional religious practises. However, forcing women to unveil denies public manifestations of Muslim presence and far from liberating covered women, subordinates them by mobilising the myth that women's freedom is ensured by a sexualised female form and that uncovering is moving from the margins into the desirable mainstream (Abraham, 2007). Were women to think about the compulsory nature of their own dress code, perhaps their sense of superiority would be contained (Brown, 2006).

The judicialisation of politics has particularly affected the politics of religious difference. Judicialisation has strengthened the rise of constitutional and international courts and the movement of controversies from the political to the judicial field. So, local burka disputes have become disrupted in two ways: first, through transference from the political into the judicial fields and, second, by moving from local to national and finally to transnational arenas. As judicialisation has narrowed the way disputes about the burka are framed, legal templates have adopted this standardised language so that socio-legal dynamics completely frame the spread of burka bans (Hirschl, 2008; de Galembert and Koenig, 2014). The environment where women in the street are harassed and stripped of their headscarves has become normalised, creating a growing sense of insecurity for Muslim women whose visibility makes them particularly susceptible to Islamophobic incidents (Ati, 2019). Judicial human rights have jettisoned their role as audience and neutral arbiter in favour of complying unreflectingly with techniques of control and processes of normalisation. Far from protecting a small minority of covered women, they have been mobilised to exclude them and render them vulnerable to abuse.

Thus, the way human rights are articulated by national governments banning the veil is to claim that freedom does not mean you have the right to act according to your individual will but rather in alliance with real social preconditions. The veiled Muslim woman is not seen as subject to human rights because she recalls the nomadic culture of Muslims and their loyalty to the global ummah over and above loyalty to the state. State surveillance and disciplinary tactics exercised on the bodies of its citizens, particularly those perceived as resistant to the modernist ideology undergirding its sovereignty, are called to mind when veiled women become embroiled in the state's struggle for power over bodies so that they are turned into subjects of the state rather than religiously/culturally observant (Behiery, 2013). Human rights' protection is therefore based on a secular idea of womanhood and the undressed woman as a symbol of freedom and public safety. So human rights do not unconditionally protect the vulnerable covered woman. On the grounds of emancipating them, Muslim women's protections from human rights depend on their giving up external manifestations of their religion that are deemed incompatible with the rights and freedoms of others. Allying with the politics of exception and unease makes the ECtHR guilty of securitising veiled women whose embodied practises in the public sphere have never posed an actual threat to public order (Ati, 2019). Through a combination of security fear and available technology, anyone who defies surveillance is automatically a security risk.

While human rights institutions are considered resilient to outside pressures (Petrov, 2020), it is clear from these cases that virtuous, supra-national institutions such as human rights ones are as able as national governments to engage in reactionary securitisation measures by failing in their essential role of checking excessive state power as a neutral audience. Rather, in times of heightened national security, the Court ceases to be a neutral arbiter and a check on state power and instead contributes to removing protections from vulnerable minorities. Initiatives designed to ensure that it is immune to national, strategic influences have not worked because the principle of subsidiarity as well as procedural embeddedness and geopolitical strategies of member states have combined to ensure considerable deference to national considerations. This is particularly the case when it comes to the matter of national security and alleged (however innocent) threats to it. It has been recognised that the Court will use its margin of appreciation leniently (Madsen, 2018).

Judicial human rights' embrace of national security politics marks a sharp departure from cosmopolitan ideals whose commitment to openness and tolerance of diversity sits uneasily with disproportionate securitisation of vulnerable groups. The Court's decision-making exposed how it had unreflectingly accepted national security agendas by parroting the view that full-face covering prevented the possibility of living together and disrupted the public order. While human rights are supposed to protect citizens from national state violations, in these cases the Court complied unquestioningly with governmental rhetoric, showing a lack of sensitivity to the complexities of wearing the veil, the various reasons why women might choose to cover, ignoring evidence of the exercise of choice by the litigants, and thus denying the claimants agency as women.

The ECtHR, in these cases at least, has bought into popular conceptions of unwanted bodies when security politics are heightened at the national level. Higher court decisions are especially important political signals in regions (like western Europe) where judiciaries are viewed as neutral and non-political. However, judicial human rights have become part of security politics and institutions which are held to have a morally superior role to the nation-state and a check on the powers of the nation-state have become securitising agents. This supports the view that legal rights are unreachable for marginalised groups and not enough to improve such groups' lives by failing to mitigate without resolving exploitative and discriminatory practises. The progress they offer is limited and tied up with the establishment by drawing a boundary around and thus containing rights' claims. Human rights, designed to empower, can end up enhancing elite power at the expense of the vulnerable (Brown, 2000).

The failure to probe securitisation and security practices creates insecurity through practises of normalisation and exclusion contributes to bodily precarity. Elites' rhetoric and visible security preparations have a stronger effect on public perceptions if the threat is perceived as direct and on-the-ground. If there is someone portrayed as threatening in people's locality, whom they might even pass in the street, this will fulfil this direct-threat function. Political leaders or the media might label normal behaviour a security problem to justify the implementation of policies to contain this constructed threat, and one way of conceptualising security is as being constructed in an institutional context where practises of security create insecurity through a dialectical process involving the normalisation of exclusionary practises (Kreide, 2019).

In Europe, Muslim communities defy surveillance because they live and worship separately, often speak a non-local second language and cannot easily be penetrated by informers (as earlier 'subversive' groups, like communists and anti-nuclear campaigners, could). Covered Muslim women are generally even harder to observe than men – this allows them to be portrayed as even more dangerous, more likely to be radicalised and harder to detect when they are. In its judgements, the Court mobilised orientalist conceptions of Muslim women (Skeet, 2009) displaying a connection between securitisation and coloniality. These securitising moves echo how whole populations had to be subdued and regulated to prevent uprisings – part of which involved regulation of the colonial, exotic, body (Said, 1979) and repeated in the current censuring of the veiled woman across Europe. While being couched in the language of national security and gender oppression, the overall process represents an ongoing effort to regulate markers of the colonial body as a way of continuing a neo-colonial politics in a post-colonial world at a time of heightened insecurity. The obsession with the veil is rooted in the colonial experience as a way of differentiating the civilised West and barbaric East (Baldi, 2018). By sanctioning the regulation of the Muslim woman's body, human rights law has failed to question this neo-colonial agenda in the name of preserving national security and preventing gender oppression.

Reflecting on the relationship between securitisation theory, feminism and post-colonialism, colonial relations are critical to identifying the voices that can or cannot be heard, those that are silenced or listened to. What follows from these developments is a demonstration of how Western countries have a monopoly over securitising processes from which, arguably, sub-altern countries are denied access to because it is their populations that are marginalised and silenced (Bertrand, 2018). It does not follow from this, however, that securitisation theory is complicit with the subordination of some populations. To the contrary, it is a useful intellectual framework to consider how non-Western bodies have their rights removed. The emphasis here is on European institutions that are supposed to deal with constrictions on the rights of others but have, in the new security era, moved away from this role despite being lobbied by audiences such as human rights NGOs – such as Amnesty International – that lobby the Court to hold states to account rather than defer to them. In contemporary post-colonial Europe, a new kind of exceptionalism has developed that condones virtuous racism which, in France in particular, stigmatises French people who have roots in colonialism, positing as undesirable the garçon arabe and the veiled woman as bad Muslims and the beurette and the secular Muslim as good Muslims – reflecting an extreme form of republicanism that singles out difference to sustain a soft regime of oppression (Guénif-Soulimans, 2006).

Chapter 4

THE CONDITIONALITY
OF HUMAN RIGHTS

So, far from being universal and equally applied, human rights are conditional. They are inaccessible to some marginalised, vulnerable groups whose
need for protection is especially pressing. The Court's upholding of national
bans sends a clear message that covered Muslim women cannot get protections from judicial human rights to express their religious identity in the secular public space. An obvious reason for this is their ambiguous citizenship
status – Muslim women acting religiously in a secular context are disrupting
the social order and deemed unacceptable citizens despite their formal citizenship status. This partly reflects the fraying of sovereignty and narrower
and more isolationist thinking, rendering citizenship more fragmented than
cosmopolitan, obeying a hierarchy of statuses regardless of formal membership so that some groups do not enjoy full citizenship or access to human
rights protections (Benhabib, 2004). Talk about human rights trumping
national citizenship and the latter being less relevant in the new global environment after the end of history era was precipitate: There has been no level-
ling out of justice, but a multiplication of status groups holding varying rights,
where a hierarchy of statuses means that super-citizens' access is guaranteed,
whereas marginal, quasi, sub and un-citizens have uncertain or negligible
rights (Nash, 2009).

Judicial human rights in Europe have hijacked national security agendas
that have embedded this unequal access to human rights – especially for
those asserting religious freedom – excluding certain minorities from being
rightful members of a particular polity. The fusing of citizenship and human
rights protections has been reversed by a rigid boundedness so that all it takes
to disrupt the potential political and legal connection between citizenship and
human rights is a national security crisis which mobilises securitisation processes that exclude some groups – those constructed as a threat – from basic
rights (Banai and Kreide, 2017). The ECtHR's refusal to protect Muslim
women stems from the existential insecurity of European Union (EU) member states created by insecurities accompanying national and supra-national

conflicts, which have been absorbed by the Court, exempting it from the erosion of citizenship (Heindl, 2017). This existential insecurity provides fertile soil for the revival of paternalistic nationalism, which, as we have seen, routinely regulates dress, and especially targets women thought to undermine national identity. The ECtHR has failed to challenge the tight regulation and management of religious dress, particularly in countries such as France whose old animosity towards Catholicism as backward has been replaced with a similar hostility towards Islam (Laborde, 2012). European governments' weak status underpins judicial human rights' denial of the right to religious expression in public spaces because observant Muslim women are considered dangerous citizens rather than deserving (European) ones (Ati, 2019). The ideal New Europe ranks Western identity over Islam, now seen as an internal threat, such that Muslims occupy the role of denizens – potential carriers of terrorism whose rights should be contained and sustained by a renewed notion of them as nomadic barbarians (Turner, 2016).

Thus, the most virtuous of rights have become implicated in the rise of right-wing populism across Europe. While the isolationist and anti-universalist character of populism makes it a natural enemy of human rights, judicial versions have not resisted the populist trend. Instead of protecting people from populism, human rights courts have adopted the populist, isolationist and increasingly authoritarian rhetoric of governments. In the clash between majoritarian rights and minority rights, virtuous institutions do not have the tools to counter populism and are pressured into giving way to domestic considerations, encouraged by domestic attempts to remedy (or not) human rights issues that silence supra-national organisations. Populism has therefore eroded the authority of Courts such as the ECtHR, partly because of their foundational function and also because of the nature of judicial personnel, where the elite status of judges acts as a basis for links with national elites who adhere to populism. The ECtHR only has as much authority as national governments allow, and while there is some progress towards greater diversity amongst judges, old patterns remain entrenched (Dzehtsiarou and Schwartz, 2020). While judicial selection is complex, those appointed to Courts are not likely challengers to state authority but are part of the establishment to which heads of national government belong and judges' ideology is tied to the political ideology of the governments that appointed them. So, national sovereignty is never far away and leads to policy pragmatism (Voeten, 2007). The European Convention's origins relate to attempts by older EU members to protect the Union from slipping back into totalitarian politics of new member states, so in heightened national security the Court's independence is limited, predisposing it towards an expansion of the subsidiarity principle and margin of appreciation (Kratochvíl, 2011).

What is clear is that supra-national institutions are operating in a new post-democratic world which has seen the rise of populist figures such as Trump, Erdogan, El-Sisi and Bolsonaro (Roth, 2017). Now they are operating in the context of an unprecedented rise of right-wing versions of populism in France, Italy, Hungary, Germany, the United Kingdom and even more unlikely countries such as Sweden, where there has been a movement towards white melancholia (Hübinette and Lundström, 2011). Popular support for the Danish People's Party, the Norwegian Progress Party, the Swiss People's Party and the Freedom Party in the Netherlands has grown. The right-wing coalition led by Giorgi Meloni's Brothers of Italy party won a clear majority in the 2022 Italian election. And it seems that human rights institutions have been unable or unwilling to stand up to widespread opposition to their laws and the right to hold governments to account. The paradox of Courts such as the ECtHR allying with populism's outright hostility to human rights has led to their acceptance rather than challenge the idea that Muslims are a threat to common European values – a thread that runs through right-wing populist parties driving the veiling ban and presenting the veil as anti-democratic. The irony being that populism's cultural framing of such a simple piece of clothing is couched in terms of a clash between the people and a cosmopolitan elite intent on undermining the nation (Yilmaz, 2012).

The Court's compliance with national bans on the veil and the disregard for Muslim women's rights by conceding to national governments' regulation of clothing – women's in particular – exposes how, when in a state of national existential crisis, it is inclined towards toeing governmental lines. They are seeking a homogenous public space where people whose habits depart from the majority's come to have their citizenship rights eroded in a futile effort to establish order in a disordered world (Baldi, 2018). Targeting the Muslim woman – however innocent – was one way to stem an unravelling, overarching European identity, and the ECtHR failed to end this excessive regulation of Muslim women to the extent of sanctioning their forcible unveiling. They adopted a policy which placated popular prejudice to the detriment of human rights' essential commitment to protecting human dignity (Ati, 2019) and, in doing so, endorsed populist Islamophobia.

Underlying this deference to national governments and populism is the new security environment that propelled governments to adopt excessive securitisation measures in a new geopolitical environment of unpredictable terrorist acts happening inside rather than outside Europe (Cronin, 2002). This saw the construction of a new, dangerous citizen: the home-grown terrorist. This new enemy coincided with the 2015 refugee crisis so that supra-national entities such as the EU used strategic emergency controls, border controls and surveillance which ran alongside intra-European conflict over refugee and immigration policies (Morsut and Kruke, 2018). This environment meant that judicial human rights bought into past residues of racism characterised by a long-standing prejudice against Muslims (Balibar, 1991) where Muslims are portrayed as disloyal citizens based on ideas about a new form of desert violence that saw Islam as theologically reactionary and part of populism's distancing from antisemitism for a more popular form of racism (Hafez, 2014). Human rights institutions failed to check national governments' efforts to appease an electorate already steeped in popular anti-Muslim prejudice, making themselves useful to populist parties such as Marine Le Pen's, who dropped the antisemitic ideology of her party's past in favour of a new racism directed almost exclusively against Muslims. Her attack on the headscarf is a calculated step to refocus from Jews as the enemy within to Muslims. Paradoxically, progressive movements have aligned with populists on this matter, enabling the political success of a populist agenda (Göle, 2017b).

More fundamentally, the bans and counter protests have torn up the perceived wisdom that Islam would dissolve as Muslims became part of modernity. In fact, the division between secularism and religion has become more blurred as Europe's Muslims have asserted their position in the public sphere by performing their religion in new ways. Now, there is no going back to the long-held idea that secularisation accompanying modernisation in the European context would reveal Islam as a backward religion. Now that Islam is no longer confined to Muslim-majority countries but has acquired a presence in Europe, it is impossible to continue to retain such stereotypical views. Yet, while Islam's relationship with Europe has become increasingly intimate, it has also become more confrontational (Göle, 2012) which drives greater securitisation and surveillance of Muslim citizens, especially those displaying their religious allegiance.

Even more controversially, human rights' complicity in regulating the Muslim woman's body is grounded in their weddedness to liberal Western feminism which has allied itself with this populist turn as both feminists and the far right deprecate Muslim women's dress and engage in national governments' routine parade of testimonial figures of the ideal Muslim woman, such as Ayaan Hirsi Ali and Fadela Amara (a French Algerian whose support for the ban on the burka represented it as comparable with fascism and undemocratic),[1] to argue in favour of bans on covering by using Muslim women such as Amara because she adheres to Republican values that refuse to accommodate the veil (Amiraux, 2013; Fernando, 2009). Human rights denial of Muslim women's freedom to cover stems from a deep-rooted

---

1 https://fcc.uchicago.edu/directory/neither-whores-nor-submissive-burqa-ban-france.

commitment to a liberal notion of sexual citizenship which proposes that a true sexual citizen regards religion as backward, repressed or primitive. This form of citizenship denies entry into democratic modernity to women unless they conform to Western norms, such that the inclusivity of human rights is reined in and adopts an exclusionary position on various subgroups – mainly Muslim women – who are portrayed as victims of their own culture, considered incompatible with Western justice (Sabsay, 2012).

European case law displays a paternalistic nationalism that views covering as an infringement of Muslim women's right to be people amongst people, thus denying them agency while buying unreflectingly into the idea they are a security threat (Bilge, 2010). Human rights' opposition to Muslim women's dress rests on the untested belief that they are protecting women from abuse. If judicial human rights could free themselves from the grip of national governments, they could disrupt the hard religious/secular boundary and abandon the rescue narrative so obvious in case judgements. The Court's decision-making can be likened to the knee-jerk debates that emerged when feminism from the South denounced Western feminists for their uncritical colonial attitudes and for being unwilling to contemplate an alternative view of gender and to abstract from the patronising colonial notion of white men saving brown women from brown men (Sabsay, 2012). By allying unthinkingly with Western liberal feminism, human rights have implicated themselves in the double standards about women's bodies embedded in our culture where judges and public policy makers are given a right to control how women should appear in public: over-dressed and under-exposed or under-dressed and over-exposed. Women who are thought to be wearing too much are called upon to undress on the grounds that they are either oppressed or dangerously interfering with the rights of others; whereas, women thought to be wearing too little are told to dress themselves lest they invite sexual assault or look like prostitutes. When considered in this way, we can see more clearly how odd judicial and public regulation of women's clothing is (Beaman, 2013).

The Court's approach to Muslim dress also reveals the limits of left legalism and cause lawyering to pressure the Court into maintaining its foundational commitment to bodily integrity. Left legalism has been trying to give voice and agency to women affected by the burka bans by appealing to freedom of religion and multiculturalism as a way of accommodating religious pluralism. The unintended consequence of this is that it engages in processes which shape the act of veiling without reference to the multiple ways in which women might choose to cover and fails to see that the ban does not simply silence women but wholly constitutes the Muslim woman. It is not, therefore, necessarily an effective way of combatting state power and decentralising it (Fournier, 2013). Litigation by Muslim women has failed to penetrate this process and expose how this form of left legalism's scope for rallying behind individual cases has (at least in Europe) been limited. Muslim women cannot rely on the left to force human rights law to ensure justice through legal means as promised by the liberal state.

These failures reflect the difficulties encountered by progressive movements that have increasingly relied on legal channels to implement, for example affirmative action or protection against sexual harassment – the result of which is a form of political disunification, which can only be partially remedied by observation of the effects of such engagement (Brown and Halley, 2002). The formal, legalistic approach to asserting and defending their rights has led to negative outcomes because the law – especially human rights law – is a slow and blunt instrument. Cases concerning Muslim dress are forced upwards to supra-national courts, which are supposed to act as a neutral arbiter to state power and yet, when dealing with alleged national security matters, deliver negative verdicts which invariably push back into a national jurisdiction, where (majority) cultural norms shape the law and its interpretation. Judicial human rights in Europe are coloured by a multitude of problems which might affect women's rights. As we have seen, applications are declared inadmissible or there may be disproportionate derogation of provisions in national emergencies or deferral to national states in public security. Thus, judicial human rights instrumentalised through the ECtHR have become embroiled in the securitisation process normally ascribed to national institutions and actors (Dembour, 2006), jettisoning the role of neutral audience.

In the new national security environment, human rights have failed to be a proper audience, allowing instead the exclusion of certain categories of citizens deemed to be threats to national security, however fictional, in deference to national sovereignty. Technically, this has been facilitated by the principle of subsidiarity leading, in this case, the ECtHR to heighten rather than protect women's bodily vulnerability. The bureaucratic constraints, the networking with national governments and the elite composition of human rights judges in Europe mean that, when necessary, the visionary reach of such virtuous rights is reined in. This human rights paradox rests on how they relate to politics. Far from providing an effective challenge to established patterns of power relations, judicial human rights have solidified them. This is because those who make rights claims are not targeting their claims at overall injustices but at very specific claims which, if remedied, leave inequality intact. This speaks about the difficulties of identity politics and rights claims that abound in this area. While one cannot deride calls to improve the conditions in which various marginalised groups live – such as refugees or asylum seekers (and in this case, Muslim women) – the question of deeper, more radical change becomes redundant (Douzinas, 2013; Moyn, 2018).

At a deeper level, the Court's decision-making reflects an engrained ambivalence within human rights where they are the benchmark of security and insecurity and whose conditionality can be traced to their alignment with neo-liberalism, which has led them to neglect structural inequalities within and between nations, rendering them more or less empty, which suggests a need to shift their attention from identity to underlying structures of privilege and under-privilege, given that the possession of rights still lies mainly with property ownership, held by a very small number of politically powerful elites (Moyn, 2018). Human rights are committed from the outset to a normative individualism that centres on the protection of individual security, which makes it difficult for them to accommodate the idea of a community within a community. The use of human rights to uphold national bans on the veil exposes a tension between universalist and communitarian principles such that 'liberalism's poorly drawn fight with communitarianism [lacks] a strong account of solidarity', where communitarianism is understood as an 'enemy or at least a foil'. The liberal idea of rights needs to include recognition of communal, especially religious, identities. Without this, they are indecisive in combatting securitisation – being simultaneously conditions for freedom and resistance and instruments of oppression. Women's rights are integral to this as they presume the (baseless) persona of suspect terrorist based on a visibility of the supposed gulf between the West and the Rest, which leads to the instrumentalisation of women's rights for the purpose of security (Kreide, 2019).

The appearance of a common purpose between human rights and citizenship remains a deceit and exposes how the legacy of liberal individualism, which underscores both, provides the basis for incompatibility between the boundedness of the nation and the supposed openness of human rights (Nash, 2009). The paradox of judicial European human rights is that they are based on both resistance and containment and a normative liberalism concerned with individual security and not that of communities. This failure has its roots in classical theory, in the views of Locke and Montesquieu and the dominant status of natural law (Kreide, 2019). John Stuart Mill's (1949 [1859]: 75) summary statement 'Of the limits to the authority of society over the individual' conveys this liberal ambivalence, as much through its convolution as its conclusion:

> Everyone who receives the protection of society owes a return for the benefit, and the fact of living in society renders it indispensable that each should be bound to observe a certain line of conduct towards the rest. This conduct consists, first, in not injuring the interests of one another; or rather certain interests, which, either by express legal provision or by tacit understanding, ought to be considered as rights; and secondly, in

each person's bearing his share (to be fixed on some equitable principle) of the labour and sacrifices incurred for defending the society or its members from injury or molestation.

These principles continue to guide contemporary human rights law. Now it is about the exercise of life, liberty, property and security. The major problem, however, is that freedom does not include the potential for social participation. The normative liberalism to do with protecting individual security is based on being a part of mainstream society. There is a tension between human rights and participation in a community rooted in the liberal tradition, which pits the individual against the others (Kreide, 2019).

The relationship between economic liberalism and international human rights has weakened their potential because they are subordinate to neo-liberalism, sitting comfortably and unquestioningly with some of the worst levels of inequality. Human rights have principally served the rich rather than the vulnerable and sustained structural injustices and inequalities, keeping the liberal order safe (Moyn, 2018). Neo-liberalism has compromised the meaning of rights as everything is reduced to the market, which means that civic and political life are understood as market spheres, so that civil and political liberties have lost their intrinsic meaning and to empower those who do not have power, in favour of capital rights (Cruz and Brown, 2016). This relationship highlights the paradox of rights and how they mitigate rather than resolve the exploitation of vulnerable, marginalised groups, even to the extent of playing a part in the governance of marginalised groups, which dilutes their potential for empowering the socially vulnerable. Human rights have therefore contributed to women's subordination, which is written in liberal jurisprudence (Brown, 2020) and which explains why Muslim women's bodily vulnerability has not been resolved. The legal outcomes reviewed here have shown how unvirtuous virtuous institutions can be when decision-making has sanctioned the denigration of Muslim women's rights and enabled the veil to become the object of a new regime of state control. State regulation, based on fear of political radicalism, ignores the multiple reasons why women choose to cover, and in doing so, essentialises expressions of Islamic religious identity as a form of resistance and threat.

Combined – the fragmentation of citizenship, populism, Western liberal feminism and commitment to individual liberalism – expose how European human rights are hamstrung by the legacy of colonialism, post-colonialism and neo-colonialism, which has led to dilution of the power of these most virtuous of rights. The sediments of this powerful legacy are iterated and reiterated in rights talk and case law that has led, contrary to their foundational vision, to a casting out of races, women and other members of humanity's hierarchy.

This legacy sits easily with rather than against the proliferation of human rights treaties or growth of institutions such as the ICC or the UN Human Rights Committee, which are embedded in deep, exploitative structures and a Western liberalism which systematically privileges some groups over others. Judicial human rights, despite their commitment to a cosmopolitan ethic, are revealing how rightlessness continues to trap marginalised groups. Rights' conditionality can in part be traced back to an orientalist hangover which results in ghettoisation to the banlieues in France and a disconnection from social and legal services (Samson, 2020). Azoulay's (2019) conception of rights treaties as fetishised texts based on embedded colonial thought appears particularly pertinent to explaining the conditionality of rights. Rights have, historically, been gifted or removed from vulnerable groups, including hard cases of disabling rights (e.g. removing land rights from indigenous populations) to softer cases of guaranteeing civil and political rights. That religious minorities have a textual right to express their religious identity is a conditional one: one that is both given and removed when the time is right. And human rights have been ineffective in protecting a soft right because, in the end, they are the servants of national sovereignty and national ideas of public order, how to be a civilised woman, and securitisation measures of suspect communities, however innocent they might be.

Where there is an environment centred around high levels of national security, judicial human rights have failed to protect the most vulnerable. This is especially clear in the hardest of cases, as in countries with authoritarian regimes engaged in counter-terrorist activities. For example, supra-national justice and bodies' willingness or ability to confront violating countries has been minimal in the ECtHR's approach to Turkey's violations of Kurdish rights, where lawyers working for abducted, executed, tortured and displaced civilians under emergency rule have largely failed, despite Turkey being a signatory to the ECtHR (Kurban, 2020). The rise of mass surveillance and an almost constant state of emergency undermines social democracy and disempowers citizens and non-citizens. Krasteva (2020) poignantly observes that the world hinges on the wall and the body, where some bodies are unwelcome and others deserving of rights. It was witnessing the catastrophic effects of the state of emergency in post-9/11 United States that enabled a democratic country to break international human rights law with impunity, which led theorists such as Agamben (2005) to abandon humanitarianism and human rights in favour of post-humanism. He noted the vicious circle that seemed to mark the end of social democratic norms, values and law, leading to an overemphasis on the politics of enemies; an over-production of enemies as security threats and a proliferation of borders between friends and enemies rooted in the bordering-othering-ordering triad. States of emergencies enable excessive management of minorities and refugees, and in this context, particular bodies are picked out as threats without foundation. This is how elites in the United States and Europe – albeit political, intellectual or from the media – protract neo-colonialism through new forms of governance, which create insecurity ideas about risk that have been created by elite and privileged actors (Huysmans, 2005).

This review of soft cases of securitisation – governing religious dress in Europe – has led us to query whether judicial human rights in Europe and elsewhere will ever fulfil the role of neutral audience and arbiter, holding national governments to account, for the sake of protecting bodily integrity. So far, we have seen that security politics have outplayed human rights and led them to fail in their foundational role: to protect the body. Liberal democracies appear blind to the incongruity between their principles and economic and political alliances with countries such as Saudi Arabia, Bahrain and China, whose human rights records are dismal. The limits of European human rights are illustrated by countries' leaders condemning the death of Jamal Khashoggi, while simultaneously facilitating ongoing trade relations with Saudi Arabia. Moreover, Britain's more peaceful process of decolonisation did not result in any flattening or reordering of the hierarchy of human rights, demonstrated by the costs paid by refugee victims of the United Kingdom's hostile environment policy and the tragedy of Grenfell Tower. Governments admit the clash between rights rhetoric and past behaviour by hiding or destroying revealing documents. Failure to acknowledge the past remains entrenched, with elites of all political persuasions tending to advocate moving on rather than meaningfully compensating for past extractive interventions. Institutions such as the UN and the ICJ are ineffectual against such entrenched disparities in rights and how revered institutions reflect an extant Eurocentrism, as when the British Museum refuses to repatriate valuable possessions removed from former colonies (Samson, 2020).

CONCLUSION: DESECURITISING HUMAN RIGHTS

However insightful these observations are, we should go beyond fatalism. We must look for answers about how vulnerable women's (and other) bodily rights might be secured. This demands a look at the public sphere's relationship to human rights' realisation. Democracy depends on a space where legitimate dissent is visible and full participation in public life is facilitated (Habermas, 1991). However, a procedural approach (proposed by Habermas) is too limiting when it comes to religion. Religion poses a particular problem for this conception of the public sphere because of the confusion around the assumption that while religion and churches are in the public domain and we need to listen to them, religious groups must use the language of the secular public space. In secular countries, this transforms those who visibly identify with an outcast religion into second-class citizens and bypasses the fact that religion is not merely a collection of beliefs but a way of life. Identifying with a religion – and expressing this through dress – is a communal activity. There are Muslims and Jews who might practise in communal religious activities without sticking precisely to the word of the Quran or Bible. We need to turn this idea on its head and propose that the public sphere needs to adjust to recognise manifestations of religious identities. We need to go beyond this dichotomy to ensure that Western universalism does not reject women's dress, hence human dignity, by erasing and assimilating Muslim woman, and to challenge why institutional religion had to retreat to the private sphere to accommodate Western modernity. Its removal from the political realm explains why new religions are now mobilising to reclaim the public sphere (Butler, 2012). Human rights are a potential tool for protecting women's bodily precarity but are limited by their Western-centric commitment to a private–public divide (Nussbaum, 2005).

In this era of dissent and difference, Göle (2017b) asks whether a genuine European public sphere that recognises diversity is in the making or the unmaking? That is, can it be a viable public sphere for people identifying openly with religious practises or not? There are clear adverse signs, as we have seen the rise of Islamophobia and the rise of the far right, often the main carriers of opposition to practises such as veiling. Dysfunctional public spheres are characterised by the exclusion of bodies deemed undeserving – the migrant or the unassimilated Muslim woman – and considered worthless as perceived threats or disruptors to one's lifestyle. The dysfunctional practise of Islamophobia is manifest daily in instances such as using the image of covered woman holding the pig to intimidate Muslims and pulling headscarves from women's heads as they walk in the street or standing over them and forcing them to remove clothing. Such actions are the most brutal of public signifiers, creating the conditions for ambient fear of others which is about boundary maintenance, a commitment to No Entry/enclave politics and casting unwanted bodies out of the city (Bauman, 2000). Such a dystopia, already real, creates an uncivil public sphere and incivility in public spaces focusses on neo-populist manifestations of Islamophobia in countries across Europe, where some groups routinely face toxic practises justified by the mythically commendable principle of absolute freedom of speech (Göle, 2017a).

How do unwanted bodies occupy their rightful place in the public sphere? Ultimately, it is about vulnerable groups owning a visibility to combat their precarity. Unwanted minority bodies are invisible unless and until they act to demand recognition through visibility and engage in political participation until they are seen. That is, to recognise the only way to combat imposed precarity is through visibly demanding equality and forcing the majority to view unwanted bodies as equal. This view echoes Arendt's (2004 [1949]) notion that an authentic public sphere is one where people come out of the shadows and make themselves visible and, so, through that performative action, become active public citizens. There is, in doing this, a kind of heroism in actions. This is about crossing from the backstage to the front-stage, moving from the private to the public, and when Muslims conduct their everyday acts of piety in the front-stage, through prayer or covering, they are ensuring that they can be seen by others and, ultimately, respected (Göle, 2017a).

For a functioning civil public sphere to be fulfilled, we need a new commitment to pluralism that abandons the idea of unwanted bodies. Constructive pluralism has surfaced in innumerably small but compelling ways. For example, in Germany, alliances have been forged between the Jewish community and Muslims, particularly significant because of Germany's history, where Jewishness has long been a visible facet of the public sphere, to the extent that European identity has been defined in a Judeo-Christian frame. So, while Judaism as a public religion has been accepted as part of Germany's postwar history, this has not been the same for Islam. However, there are religious practises – such as halal and circumcision – where there is congruence between Islam and Judaism (Göle, 2011) and around which solidarity can be created. The public sphere should be about the politics of appearance such that the absence of appearance and familiarisation renders it invalid. There must, therefore, be creative accommodation. There is evidence of this working in the field of art, such as, for example, the Jewish Museum's exhibition 'Snip it' in Berlin following the Charli Hebdo attacks, where Muslims were invited. We have, therefore, to move from a mediated public sphere to one that is based on real-life situations. Thus, for Göle (2017a) this means patience and reflexivity and working from the ground up. Despite examples such as the exhibition in Berlin, Islam has typically been signified by the media to the extent that Muslims are looking at themselves through the media rather than interacting with others so that they can be themselves and compel others to dismiss mediated portrayals.

There is growing evidence of pluralism within Islam in the European context, stemming from mixed ethnicities and nationalities through migration out of Muslim-majority countries. Extremism and Islamic fervour run alongside a blurring of traditions, for example, between Shia and Sunni Islam. Europe provides a space for this blurring because there is no possibility of an Islamic State. So, when we think about European Islam, it is important to move beyond thinking in terms of state and more about lifestyles. Islam used to be in Arabic. Iranians and Turks were seen as bad Muslims because of this. Now, in Europe, they bring Turkish language into mosques. In the United Kingdom, mosques are for British Muslims with Pakistani heritage. So, plurality is manifest in multiple ways, not Sunnism or Shi'a. In Europe, there is an opportunity for Islamic cosmopolitanism, which is a very different form of pluralism. That is why European governments try to cut off countries of origin as a form of governance. However, European Muslims have answered this by Imams presenting themselves as theologians above all, undermining the image of them as carriers of radicalism. They are young theologians who are France-born/Italy-born Muslims. They try to understand their own religion in relation to other religions.

We now see Islam and Europe relating to each other in novel ways, transforming the meaning of modernity because the predicted decline of Islam in Europe did not happen (Göle, 2012). This transformation means that Muslim women's bodies could become increasingly part of everyday life and subjected to less surveillance. The solution, from this perspective, is Europe, which provides a privileged site for exploring how modernity might change through the new interaction between religious and secular communities. Europe offers the chance to collapse temporal and spatial boundaries between Islam and the West, so that they become friends rather than enemies. While this sounds Eurocentric, it is a way of undoing standard Eurocentric narrations of modernity and recognising that the orientalist critique is less relevant when the spatial distance between cultures is narrowing, facilitated by mutual (though not equal) cultural exchange.

The project of desecuritising human rights depends, in part, on exposing their synchronous links with colonialism and neo-liberalism. If rightlessness remains structurally embedded, and citizenship rights are curtailed, the unwillingness of the elite to render them meaningful will remain entrenched. Since formal legal channels have been found wanting, rights mobilisation should be used not on its own but in conjunction with other approaches that do not depend on formal, legal challenges. This new politics of rights involves a retreat from the formal judiciaries in favour of a political movement that invokes human rights language to forge a connection with people's shared experience, ultimately showcasing human rights to the wider community (Scheingold, 2010). It falls then to intellectuals, social movements and NGOs who can work to demonstrate to the establishment the need to recognise the past hypocrisies that have characterised human rights and lobby to correct these by safeguarding customs and traditions. This has been achieved, albeit symbolically, with the removal of the statue of Cecil Rhodes amongst other acts. *Black Lives Matter* has had formidable success in forcing governments to recognise the mistreatment of black Americans and the way the past has surfaced in the present (Samson, 2020).

We need to find political and economic ways to minimise precarity and challenge the idea that vulnerability and resistance are unrelated and replace top-down control with collective resistance. Thinking about precarious bodies in countries as distinct as Turkey, Palestine and France, which are often the site of serious derogations of human rights, the message is to consider vulnerability's part in resistance. A variety of criss-crossing politics and protests can resist the most formidable forms of governance and are ultimately the source of agency based around public practises that confront power, such as the protests of mothers of the disappeared, the use of stones by Palestinians or the insistence on wearing the veil in contravention to the bans (Butler et al., 2016). Resistance can appropriate vulnerability through bodily practises in the public sphere; most recently demonstrated in Iran, as women protesters – including young girls – ostentatiously removed their veil as a challenge to the regime.

Ending corporeal management of woman-ness and sexuality in public life depends upon governance adopting a new morality and embracing inter-civilisational conversation over matters such as the headscarf. Interconnections between the public sphere, visibility and gender are critical in finding a solution that repairs the feminist divide over covering. Muslim women need to abstract themselves from state control by rejecting the ways the private is monitored by the public through a new form of public Islam, where the public sphere becomes the space for the practical performance of pluralistic identities. This might be through art - one example being the statue of a naked woman with a headscarf, titled *Turkish-Delight*, exhibited in a public garden. Such work, Göle (2017b) contends, does not depend upon discourses but nevertheless powerfully conveys the confrontation between a secular European culture and Islam. The public sphere is a space where different cultures display differences between each other through performance and practise rather than words, and in doing so, opens the opportunity for creative, friendly interaction. Hope lies with an unpacking of Eurocentric sexual norms.

Critically, we therefore also need to undo the schism between Western and post-colonial feminism. Islam itself can disturb Eurocentric conceptions of the secular public sphere and, importantly, how gender is construed in this space, and it undoes the dichotomy between Western and post-colonial feminism. Secular histories must be challenged because of their intimate relationship with Western modernity and colonialism. Now that Muslim women have insisted on entering the public sphere on their own terms, feminists have had to look again at religion. However, so far, this has been more confrontational than accommodating, with secular, universal principles espoused by European feminism winning public support. Unsettled by the sudden appearance of visible Muslim women, feminists retreated to traditional liberalism. While this began in France, moves against Muslim practises moved from this country, characterised by a strong commitment to *laïcité*, to take hold across Europe, including countries such as Denmark, and focusing on the minaret movement in more conservative countries such as Switzerland and Sharia Law in the United Kingdom. Covered Muslim women occupying a public space have been doubly discriminated against by feminists. Their new visibility has been unwelcomed with a refusal to recognise the possibility of empowerment to the extent that European feminism, adopted by judicial human rights, negates the potential authenticity of religious commitment (Göle and Billaud in Triandafyllidou et al., eds., 2011).

European feminism has so far failed to deal with Islamic difference. This is partly because secular feminists' opposition to the veil is rooted in its conflict with the power of the church which has led it to see covering as a retrograde move and diminishing the value of their post-1968 fight against church control of women's lives driven by a desire to force the church out of women's private life. The 'personal is political' axiom held that women's oppression not only applied to the public sphere but to the private too – in relation to sexuality and, of course, abortion rights. Escaping the grip of the church was thus seen as essential to the realisation of personal oppression and drove the idea that Islam was an anachronistic halt on women's agency (Göle and Billaud, in

Triandafyllidou et al., eds., 2012). Veiling has therefore exposed a deep fissure within feminism based on the rupture between Western liberal feminists and post-colonial feminists, which has thus far been unresolved. There are two clear contestations. The first is the historical backdrop to feminist opposition to the church: the veil resonates with this oppressive institution that feminists fought hard to be free from, which is particularly relevant to governance feminism. The second claims that mainstream feminism has silenced the experiences of women from the Global South (Bilge, 2010).

Signs of progress are minimal as various movements, including international human rights, have forced governments in late modern democracies to implement new juridical frames to recognise sexual diversity. This has meant that gendered others have only just begun to be included in citizenship, which proposes the formation of new sexual rights-bearing subjects. However, this apparently progressive movement has foregrounded the Western sexual citizen as a benchmark for measuring all other sexual subjects, based on marking out others according to cultural, religious and racialised differences (Sabsay, 2012). So, for real progress to be made, it is essential that we overcome the dichotomy within feminism, where, for liberal/universalist feminists, the veil is seen as a marker of subordination and oppression, and where cultural insiders such as Fadela Amara are mobilised to support their cause as experts versus post-colonialist feminists who see the veil as a form of resistance, albeit against commodification and Westernisation. Both approaches sideline the possibility of wearing the veil for religious reasons (Bilge, 2010).

Thus, Western liberal feminists or secular Muslim women need to move beyond the narrative that the veil is necessarily oppressive to women and to feel free to critique the use of French Muslim women as good Muslims who oppose the veil. Western feminists are stuck in orientalist thinking because they hold to the tired narrative about oppression of Muslim women and examples of good Muslims – that is, enlightened and emancipated - as opposed to bad Muslims, veiled or violent Arab men. A preferable analysis of Muslim dress legislation would be to consider it in relation to race in French society, its polity and the public sphere. It is important to understand the relationship of regulations on dress to the political and social subordination of people whose embodiment and enactment of religious practises are used to devalue their presence and delegitimise their participation in the polity. There is, from this view, an urgent need to examine how the racial aspects of this debate and how the state's role in it produces racialised subjects await analysis (Bilge, 2013). Acceptance of such an analysis would reframe laws that sanction the visibility of religious dress (Amiraux, 2016).

Post-colonial feminists have shown that covering can be agentic and a subversion of Western-ness and, as such, a form of resistance that challenges the civilisationist ideas within Western feminism. Western feminists must consider how far liberal democracies should accommodate difference and reflect more carefully on whether the covered Muslim woman has a legitimate claim to public space, based on a division between universalism and minority rights (Bilge, 2010). So far, these claims have not been heard. Reactions to topless Muslim feminist days to liberate women from the oppression of the hijab suggest covered women have chosen to be victims. The counter-narrative has mobilised the slogan 'Nudity does not liberate me. I do not need saving', challenging Western ideas of freedom and highlighting the racism embedded in FEMEN talk (Sabsay, 2012). Western feminism should stop re-orientalising covered women and rejecting any possibility that they are exercising choice and recognise that their rights calls come from Islam itself because Islam and rights are not necessarily antithetical (An'Naim, 2011). There needs to be recognition of the ambivalent status of Muslim women whose distancing from their backgrounds has led to their being welcomed by Western governments and feminism, but continue to have a misfit identity based on wanting to maintain their religious identity and autonomy, which means they occupy an in-between identity caused by demands from their background and an unsympathetic Western secularism.

Feminism should therefore reflect on the idealisation of the exposed body and compulsory visibility, which embeds the view of the visible face as both target and effect of governmentality. As a constructed form of civil disobedience, the veil is a new object of biometric control over individuals – it is not allowed because it disturbs surveillance technologies and enforces the notion that rightful citizens have nothing to hide and deserve protection, whereas those who conceal their hair or face are resisting progressive ideals. They are the antithesis of modernity and republicanism: images of Marianne often show her topless and with her face visible, thus embodying French national identity (Dorlin in Butler et al., 2016). With invisibility, feminists might note, comes the power of being free from surveillance and being able to look without being looked at in a hyper-corporeal, third-person way.

To counter the securitisation of the veil and the complicity of judicial human rights, we could turn to relentless rebellion rooted in the combined resistance of human rights groups, Muslim women of various persuasions, feminists, the left and anti-racists by realising that framing the bans on the veil in terms of national security and gender oppression has served to disguise the securitising agenda underpinning them and to decolonise the language of security, which has demanded assimilation and an enforced whiteness of the public space dependent on age-old regulation of women's bodies under colonialism. This kind of activism has the potential to successfully disconnect European human rights from a securitising, neo-colonial project (Brayson,

2019). For feminism, the issue is not about supporting or opposing the veil but to question why the West is so preoccupied with Muslim women's religious dress and to untangle how Western secularism enables the regulation of women's bodies in liberal democracies, ostensibly committed to human rights. Such reflection will enable a challenge to the way Islam has been cast as the antithesis of such rights through civilisational delusions that underpin legal bans on the veil. Equality for women and their freedom would be more successfully advanced by this kind of self-scrutiny, as would prospects for civil cohabitation in liberal democracies whose culturally heterogeneous character is irreversible (Brown, 2012).

However, it is intellectually limiting simply to locate all aspects of securitisation and derogation of rights within the language of decolonisation. Far more productive would be recognition of possibilities for dialogue, mutual recognition and common ground over what counts as modernity within and without the colonial mind (Táíwò, 2022). It is vital that a dialogue between human rights and political theologies takes place so that human dignity, both secular and religious, can be melded and attained. Ideas about human dignity were articulated in liberation theologies – which concerned themselves with colonialism – but also Islamic forms of feminism concerned with patriarchy. In relation to women's dress and covering, it is critical that we shift away from Western universalism where the burqa can be used to annihilate and assimilate Muslims (Santos, 2015).

The question we are left with is how human rights might be compelled to enable participation in the public sphere by minorities considered as disruptors of social cohesion. The limits of human rights can be found in how they are implicated in securitising unwanted bodies: migrants, asylum seekers or unpopular minorities who have formal citizenship. These bodies are presented by national governments as a threat to public order, social cohesion and national identity – all of which are displayed in the public sphere. It follows that common views about enemies within and without make it difficult for vulnerable groups, even those with citizenship, to enjoy the full protections offered by human rights (Ben-Porat and Ghanem, 2017). We have seen that strategic litigation is not the answer, and rights claims are restrained by the liberalism in which they are encased, so how can Muslim women express their identity in the public sphere as European citizens without suffering increased control, discipline and securitisation?

The covered Muslim woman could abstract from the political and legal security agenda by engaging in everyday micro practises instead of strategic litigation: going to work wearing the hijab or wearing it in other public spaces such as universities, cafes or restaurants. This would involve a reversal of hyper-corporality: By forcing others to see them as they see themselves, veiled women can start to create viable counter-narratives to those approved by judicial human rights and encourage human rights courts to recognise their legitimacy (Legros and Lièvre in Van Baar et al., 2019). This echoes Benhabib's (2011) exhortation for continuous iterative practises to close the gap between diversity and universal human rights. These practises must take place in the public sphere, which is a space for social solidarity to play out, where people might come together to engage in various forms of participation to defy their exclusion from it, which is an essential form of alienation (Calhoun, 2002). By acting in the public sphere, veiled women are demanding that they be recognised as a community within a community (Kreide, 2019).

For this, we could turn to the much-neglected rebellious cosmopolitanism of Camus's politics as a vehicle for rescuing human rights from their complicity in regulating the Muslim woman's body. This would involve unrelenting rebellion and strategic use of non-judicial human rights (Hayden, 2013) which could only work through making effective alliances, which are so far missing because the securitisation of the veil has such popular appeal and strategic value for governments pursuing security as part of their neo-colonial agenda. This strikes a chord with Camus' critique of neo-liberal governmentality. Originally a *pied noir* born in Algeria, his 'absurdist' awareness led him to deprecate absolute conceptions of justice and history while proposing a cosmopolitan humanism that opposed the creation of an independent Algerian nation-state (Davis, 2011). We can draw on Camus' thought on the absurdities of neo-liberalism as an important basis for critiquing human rights as they currently stand, embedded in a neo-liberal environment. The veil has the potential for resistance identity-building (Lorasdaği, 2009), but to bring it into normal politics and out of security, covered Muslim women will need to make alliances with sympathetic organisations such as *Amnesty International* and *Human Rights Watch*, both of which have consistently stated that bans on the headscarf and burka violate international human rights and representatives of which have made statements in support of the women in *SAS v. France* and the other cases and feminists are going to have to end internal divisions.

Cosmopolitan rebellion asks that Muslim women wearing various forms of covering (or removing it like in Iran) actively confront the state's regulation of their bodies. This process has transformative power because the clothing, once seen as a form of humility, becomes a symbol of defiance. State governance of women's bodies has politicised the act of wearing the veil from something personal into a public declaration that undermines the idea of the docile Muslim woman – passive objects of an authoritarian Islam. These confrontations are infinite and signal ever-growing and novel manifestations of ethno-religious identities which will compel judicial human rights to listen. Such democratic iterations are forms of rebellion and transformation that cannot be forever ignored. They provide the basis for the renegotiation of religious, cultural, legal and political meanings in the public spheres of liberal democracies. Iterations are not only simple repetitions but also the resignification of the original, which is an infinite process, undermining the idea of a fixed, authoritative meaning. Such actions, which challenge rights and other principles of the liberal-democratic state, must be articulated in the public sphere so that excluded groups are heard by multiple audiences to facilitate democratic dialogue that recognises the fluidity of rights and their jurisgenerative capacity for politics that confront religious and cultural differences. While we have not yet reached a state of civility despite ever-growing plurality of religious identities performed in public (Benhabib, 2016) the potential for this needs to be constantly repeated. It is important that relentless rebellion joins the interests of both groups and harnesses them to a common goal.

What would post-colonial justice look like? A rebellious cosmopolitanism, derived from Camus, stands on the premise of progress through solidarity, dialogue and appreciation of the stranger in oneself and in others (Hayden, 2013). Camus crosses the divide between colonial and post-colonial: his biography predisposed him to a mix of ideas that distract from the idea of a pure decolonisation of thought, which even if it were to be ideal, would be practically impossible to achieve because we can do our best to understand others, but we cannot eradicate ourselves of our own intellectual trajectories. This is healthy because it recognises the intermixing of ideas so that it becomes impossible to say some are purely European and others are purely non-European (Táíwò, 2022). An exploration of the relationship between human rights is a particularly interesting one because it exposes the duplicity of those regions that proclaim themselves to be the hub of human rights – for example, in Europe – but can also form a bridge between European thought and thought from previously colonised countries and human rights traditions within Islam. This could enable a conception of human rights that confronts the secular hegemonic version as religion increasingly makes claims on the public sphere, forcing us to recognise that human dignity is just as much a value in religion as it is in human rights. The age-old antithesis between human rights and religion needs to be dissolved so that human rights can be rescued from their colonial origins (Santos, 2015).

Camus' (1953) politics strikes a chord with the politics of vulnerability, one that hinges on the unarguable fact that our embodied vulnerability is experienced in multiple ways. The rebellions of the vulnerable have, against the tide of rising authoritarianism and populism, been successful in addressing violations of bodily integrity in Latin America, India, Russia, the United States and Europe with protests that embrace such distinct practises such as feminicide to the exploitation of care workers in Spain (Sabsay, 2020). This applies also to the anti-veiling movements in Europe and protests against forced veiling in Iran, and photography has played an important role in shining a light on all sorts of bodily violations including people smuggling and local protests against Europe's treatment of refugees from unpopular countries such as Syria, Afghanistan and Africa. All these forms of resistance are acts of human rights, from the grassroots, and their plurality amounts to solidarity which will eventually compel human rights elites to join in and act as an authentic audience.

Securitisation has created a democratic deficit that targets precarious and vulnerable people, especially Muslims and Muslim women's bodies. It has taken precedence over human rights' ostensible commitment to protecting bodily integrity, including the right to religious expression in the public sphere – where dress amounts to a second skin. Securitising measures have reinforced vulnerability, making it harder for precarious groups to protest and create embodied vulnerability criss-crossed by gender, race and age. However, these measures have been double-edged, creating a growing movement that foregrounds bodily vulnerability in their protests – often through art and other performative representations that shine a light on vulnerable bodies. Such public actions make their claims by exposing the bodies on which those claims are made. Feminist movements of varying forms have centre-staged vulnerable women's bodies to denounce gender-based violence. Such resistance has taken place in the street to ensure visibility in the public space. Resistance to securitisation is increasingly using the body as a vehicle for articulating grievances to undermine long-standing biopolitical regimes of control. A major facet of this is to expose how neo-liberal ideas of sovereign dominance are redundant by transforming political and cultural meanings and the nature of democracy itself. We have the capacity to protest without verbalisation and therefore the opportunity to do politics differently (Sabsay, 2020). This thinking echoes Butler's (2012) idea that precarity can itself galvanise protest that thrives on bodily performativity in visible protests – such as wearing the headscarf with the colours of the tricolour.

Veiling or unveiling has become a bodily act that forces human rights to recognise bodily integrity in multiple ways because of the intimate connection between clothing – the second skin – and the body. The skin might be the way a body is sensorially contained, but the body is almost invariably seen through clothing. Dress has a deeply human purpose, which is to create a self-conscious individual image, an image linked to imagined and creative visions of the human body. Claims that veiling makes women invisible ignore how veiled women can be seen and can see, and human rights should recognise how covering is a way of being visibly Muslim in a secular public sphere, which casts the veiled woman as a block on the gaze (Gökareksel and Secor, 2014) and to living together (vivre ensemble). Resilience depends upon infrastructural supports (Butler in Butler et al., 2016). By mobilising their embodied vulnerability, in the face of severe public reactions and law, covered Muslim women in secular public spaces are demanding the right for recognition and showing, at once their precarity and agency. Judicial human rights, through exposure to visible displays of bodies covered or uncovered in the public sphere, will eventually have to reconceptualise their notion of the body as merely physical to one that recognises dress as integral to human dignity. Vulnerable bodies – in this case European Muslim women – must bridge the divide between Western and post-colonial feminism to reinforce the necessary solidarity for such a transformation. Without this, human rights risks failure to acknowledge the bodily integrity of women for whom covering is a right.

Pessimism about rights talk and its hopelessness when bare life – deemed worthless – can be saved neither by citizenship nor human rights is innovative and important (Agamben, 1998, 2005). Human rights need to be treated with caution and scepticism. However, we should avoid a nihilistic trap and, rather than abandon rights altogether, start trying to make them meaningful. The key question is whether human rights can be mobilised in a counter-hegemonic way (Santos, 2015). The main myths surrounding them – namely that their current form can be construed from their history; that they have triumphed over all other ideologies; that they can be abstracted from contingent circumstances; and that they are monolithic – should not lead to their renunciation. As we have seen, the relationship between human rights and the public sphere is predominant because this underpins a critical departure from individualistic rights closely associated with neo-liberalism to a solidaristic approach based on common vulnerabilities, even if those vulnerabilities have distinct historical trajectories and political implications. This demands a new way to imagine global justice based on collective action and a political alliance of distinct communities with diverse precarious statuses (Goodale, 2022).

Protesting in the public sphere – boldly articulating embodied religious rights in the way Muslim women have – is the best way to overturn their status as objects of security politics, turning their vulnerability into resistance even if, at first, this makes them more vulnerable. It is a defiant challenge to legal structures which discriminate and refuse access to their protections (Butler, 2020). To undermine such bureaucratic restrictions, vulnerable groups will need to resist barriers to the public sphere fiercely until they become part of normal politics. This embrace of danger has been seen in Iran, where young women have mobilised against the regulatory regime while aware of the very real and frightening risks. The risks are not so great in France and other

European countries seeking to regulate women's bodies, but it is by making alliances between Western human rights and religious concepts of dignity and Western and Islamic feminism that there can be a genuine transcendence of the abyssal line (Santos, 2015). Institutional religion had to retreat to the private sphere to accommodate Western modernity, removing it from the public realm, which explains why new religious mobilisation is reclaiming the public sphere.

Human rights are meaningless if they contribute to the insecurity rather than the security of the vulnerable – at their core, they need to provide conditions for ensuring that vulnerable groups are free from governmental securitising politics. The underlying solution for solidarity based on cosmopolitan rebellion depends upon an optimum level of economic, political and juridical consensus around acceptance: once human rights are abstracted from neo-liberalism, they could potentially reach the last utopia (Moyn, 2012). But there is nothing inevitable about this: human rights are, despite their obvious failures, a work in progress, constantly open to innovation (Douzinas, 2000). There is no end as such because the search for their full realisation continues, and this creativity at the core of human rights provides grounds for optimism. Dialogue and confrontation between and within the colonial heritage of human rights mark the starting point for change. The act of wearing the veil in Europe is an example of talking back to the colonisers. It is an anti-securitising act. Appropriating rights talk as a form of politics does not mean that these women have adopted Eurocentric conceptions of rights because rights talk is also found within Islam (An'Naim, 2011). It is through these small acts that oppressed groups are expressing agency. Maybe it is European Muslims who can rescue the European judiciary from its embedded orientalism by turning the mirror onto the upholders of rights.

So far, human rights have been impotent in the face of ongoing abuse of vulnerable people such as women, indigenous groups, ethnic minorities, refugees and asylum seekers. Textual human rights, that is formal treaties, give lie to the idea that they are universally held. Notions of human inequality infuse the ideas of the architects and inheritors of the American Declaration of Independence, the French Declaration of the Rights of Man and nineteenth-century British liberals. Written into the multiple post-war treaties is a self-evident absence of the marginalised and the vulnerable. Textual human rights are flimsy and fetishised (Azoulay, 2019). Some bodies are rendered disabled by them because of their inherent imperial aspect; the absence of certain groups of people has long been commented on. Human rights, in their textual form, have excluded colonised bodies. Citizenship rights have been used against them – through, for example, granting French citizenship to Algerian Jews and Berbers to detach them from their homes (Puar, 2017). Ultimately, human rights depend upon solidaristic relationships. These can grow out of conditions of greater economic equality and movement, across and within borders, because the real success of multicultural pluralism depends upon such social causes and fails in their absence. Trust between communities can only thrive if both old and new xenophobia are eroded with the decline of social capital attached to egoistic individualism. There is a choice, therefore, between cosmopolitanism and nihilism. If mistrust of strangers thrives with conflict, we need civility and peace to put an end to assumptions that some bodies are more valuable than others – which human rights institutions have thus far failed to do (Turner, 2006)

The world is increasingly unstable – with new wars, pandemics and the rise of authoritarianism. These developments have created new sources of bodily precarity and vulnerability, which affect women and men differently. Just when we need human rights to be implemented, international bodies appear too weak to impose them. International human rights have failed to resolve deep divisions that are prominent in the media, such as the Palestinian fight for statehood, but also failed to shine a light on conflicts such as Yemen, where geopolitical interests outdo any attempt to bring this conflict out into clear view; ongoing abuse of Muslim minorities in countries such as Saudi Arabia and Europe, and Kurdish minorities amongst so many others. The Covid pandemic, which also revealed geopolitical competition to the extent that competing for sources, treatments and vaccines halted progress in tackling the disease, and in Iran, young people have been executed by a regime intent on suppressing a progressive movement. The protests against Netanyahu in Israel were a potent example of democratic activism, but simultaneously showed an unwillingness to address the Palestinian issue. And in secular countries, the human right to expose one's body in the public sphere according to religious impulses has rendered Muslim women vulnerable to state-sanctioned violence, without the protections of human rights. Far from the *Age of Rights* ushering in an era where we can count on our bodily vulnerability being protected, we have seen more examples of the failure of human rights – much of which is gendered.

Securitisation, in its hard and soft forms, can only be combatted by solidaristic alliances in the public sphere. With the rise of AI, the question must be asked: Will people stay at the top of the hierarchy or are we entering the dystopic world explored by Baxi (2009), who asks whether there are two realms of human rights: those in times of peace and those in times of conflict. Securitisation thrives in a national security context where states of exception can easily be put in place and rights derogated by social democracies as well as authoritarian governments. In a post-human world, there is an overwhelming focus on security, which threatens the foundation of human rights and the centring of the body and its protections. AI's relationship with human rights is fraught. Optimists would point to how AI has given non-state actors access to unprecedented amounts of open-source data that is verifiable. Images of abuses of authority can now routinely be observed by the amateur journalist and used as evidence against state abuses of the body. For example, the ICC issued an indictment for the arrest of a Libyan warlord based on satellite imagery and videos taken of the executions he ordered (or conducted himself), where the images were verified by triangulation (Livingston and Risse, 2019).

However, for AI not to overtake humanity and to maintain the centrality of the body, human rights must keep a tight audit on the discriminatory way it can be used, through algorithms which might enhance bodily vulnerability and states finding more ways to regulate unwanted bodies. One of the most dangerous current examples of how technology might undermine the foregrounding of living people is China's routine use of surveillance, submitting its population to unrelenting observation based on technology such as facial recognition software. Superintelligence and ever-growing threats of deepfakes, which are already underway, so that AI can appropriate a living person, pose a further risk to human rights (Livingston and Rissse, 2019). We have already noted that one of the problems with human rights is that they have too close a relationship with neo-liberalism and gross inequalities. When it comes to AI, there is a danger that this technology will heighten such inequalities as global billionaires take control of it. Those who own the economy benefit from it more than those who just work within it (Risse, 2019).

In such a potentially dystopian environment, the only way human rights can be saved from their entanglement with the structural inequalities that accompany contemporary neo-liberal politics is by the assertion of bodily rights in the public sphere. The liberatory potential of such rights can only be realised through enhanced theorising and activism (Baxi, 2009). Vulnerability can be mobilised against violence through taking a defiant place that transgresses what is deemed acceptable and by using the body as a vehicle of protest – albeit through veiling or unveiling – as well as other forms of precarity to force human rights to concede rights to marginalised, unwanted bodies. In countries such as Iran, such embodied protests carry huge risks; in others, the risks are less daunting. With transnational solidarity and alliances, these risks can be shared, and harms reduced. This kind of cosmopolitan rebellion demands a retreat from a strong version of identity politics – such as those that have divided feminism over how Muslim women dress. A hard commitment to identity politics means that difference, rightly recognised, risks playing into divide-and-rule politics that allow the powerful to maintain a grip on power that enables ongoing marginalisation of the vulnerable (Hekman, 2000). Constant rebellion depends on a universalism that accepts a mix between East and West, North and South, with different religions standing side by side with each other and with secularism as the source of global solidarity.

BIBLIOGRAPHY

Abraham, Ibrahim. 2007. 'The Veil and the Closet: Islam and the Production of Queer Space'.

Abu-Lughod, Lila. 2001. '"Orientalism" and Middle East Feminist Studies'. *Feminist Studies* 27 (1): 101–13. Edited by Meyda Yegenoglu, Zehra Arat, Homa Hoodfar, Judith Tucker, Haideh Moghissi, Ziba Mir-Hosseini, Deniz Kandiyoti, Fatima Mernissi, and Ruth V. Ward. https://doi.org/10.2307/3178451.

Agamben, Giorgio.1998.*Homo Sacer: Sovereign Power and Bare Life*.Redwood City:Stanford University Press.

———. 2005. *State of Exception*. Chicago: University of Chicago Press.

Ahmed, Sara. 2003. *Uprootings/Regroundings: Questions of Home and Migration*. Oxford: Berg.

Amir, Merav, and Hagar Kotef. 2018. 'In-Secure Identities: On the Securitization of Abnormality'. *Environment and Planning D: Society and Space* 36 (2): 236–54. https://doi .org/10.1177/0263775817744780.

Amiraux, Valérie. 2013. 'The "Illegal Covering" Saga: What's Next? Sociological Perspectives'. *Social Identities* 19 (6): 794–806. https://doi.org/10.1080/13504630.2013 .842678.

———. 2016. 'Visibility, Transparency and Gossip: How Did the Religion of Some (Muslims) Become the Public Concern of Others?' *Critical Research on Religion* 4 (1): 37–56. https://doi.org/10.1177/2050303216640399.

An-Na'im, Abdullahi Ahmed. 2011. *Muslims and Global Justice*. Philadelphia: University of Pennsylvania Press.

Arendt, Hannah. 2004. *The Origins of Totalitarianism* (1st ed.). New York, NY: Schocken Books.

Ati, Aymen. 2019. 'The Post-9/11 Securitisation of the Hijab and International Human Rights Law: The Strasbourg Court, Article 9 and Hijab Restrictions'. *SSRN Scholarly Paper*. Rochester, NY. https://papers.ssrn.com/abstract=3425845.

Azoulay, Ariella. 2019. *Potential History: Unlearning Imperialism*. London onVerso.

Baar, Huub van. 2017. 'Evictability and the Biopolitical Bordering of Europe'. *Antipode* 49 (1): 212–30. https://doi.org/10.1111/anti.12260.

Baar, Huub van, Ana Ivasiuc, and Regina Kreide. 2019. *The Securitization of the Roma in Europe*. https://doi.org/10.1007/978-3-319-77035-2.

Baldi, Giorgia. 2016. 'Liberal Paradoxes: Women's Body, Religious Expression, and Gender Equality in a Secular Age'. *AG About Gender - International Journal of Gender Studies* 5 (10). https://doi.org/10.15167/2279-5057/ag.2016.5.10.327.

———. 2018. '"Burqa Avenger": Law and Religious Practices in Secular Space'. *Law and Critique* 29 (1): 31–56. https://doi.org/10.1007/s10978-017-9208-5.

Balibar, Étienne. 1991. *Professor Emeritus of Moral and Political Philosophy Etienne Balibar, Immanuel Maurice Wallerstein, and Senior Researcher Immanuel Wallerstein. Race, Nation, Class: Ambiguous Identities.* London: Verso.

———. 2007. 'Uprisings in the Banlieues'. *Constellations* 14 (1): 47–71. https://doi.org/10.1111/j.1467-8675.2007.00422.x.

———. 2010. 'At the Borders of Citizenship: A Democracy in Translation?' *European Journal of Social Theory* 13 (3): 315–22. https://doi.org/10.1177/1368431010371751.

Balzacq, Thierry. 2005. 'The Three Faces of Securitization: Political Agency, Audience and Context'. *European Journal of International Relations* 11 (2): 171–201. https://doi.org/10.1177/1354066105052960.

Balzacq, Thierry, Sarah Léonard, and Jan Ruzicka. 2016. '"Securitization" Revisited: Theory and Cases'. *International Relations* 30 (4): 494–531. https://doi.org/10.1177/0047117815596590.

Banai, Ayelet, and Regina Kreide. 2017. 'Securitization of Migration in Germany: The Ambivalences of Citizenship and Human Rights'. *Citizenship Studies* 21 (8): 903–17. https://doi.org/10.1080/13621025.2017.1380649.

Barras, Amélie. 2009. 'A Rights-Based Discourse to Contest the Boundaries of State Secularism? The Case of the Headscarf Bans in France and Turkey'. *Democratization* 16 (6): 1237–60. https://doi.org/10.1080/13510340903271852.

Battisti, Chiara. 2016. 'Bodies, Masks and Biopolitics: Clothing as "Second Skin" and Skin as "First Clothing" in "The Tiger's Bride"'. *Pólemos* 10 (1): 101–23. https://doi.org/10.1515/pol-2016-0006.

Bauman, Zygmunt. 1997. *Postmodernity and Its Discontents.* Oxford: Polity Press.

———. 2000. 'Social Issues of Law and Order'. *The British Journal of Criminology* 40 (2): 205–21. https://doi.org/10.1093/bjc/40.2.205.

Baxi, Upendra. 2009. *Human Rights in a Posthuman World: Critical Essays.* Delhi: Oxford University Press.

Beaman, Lori G. 2013. 'Overdressed and Underexposed or Underdressed and Overexposed?' *Social Identities* 19 (6): 723–42. https://doi.org/10.1080/13504630.2013.842671.

Beck, Ulrich. 2007. 'The Cosmopolitan Condition: Why Methodological Nationalism Fails'. *Theory, Culture & Society* 24 (7–8): 286–90. https://doi.org/10.1177/0263276407024072505.

Behiery, Valerie. 2013. 'Bans on Muslim Facial Veiling in Europe and Canada: A Cultural History of Vision Perspective'. *Social Identities* 19 (6): 775–93. https://doi.org/10.1080/13504630.2013.842676.

Benhabib, Seyla. 2004. *The Rights of Others: Aliens, Residents, and Citizens.* Cambridge: Cambridge University Press.

———. 2016. 'Feminist Theory and Hannah Arendt's Concept of Public Space'. *History of the Human Sciences,* July. https://doi.org/10.1177/095269519300600205.

Ben-Porat, Guy, and As'ad Ghanem. 2017. 'Introduction: Securitization and Shrinking of Citizenship'. *Citizenship Studies* 21 (8): 861–71. https://doi.org/10.1080/13621025.2017.1380652.

Bertrand, Sarah. 2018. 'Can the Subaltern Securitize? Postcolonial Perspectives on Securitization Theory and Its Critics'. *European Journal of International Security* 3 (3): 281–99. https://doi.org/10.1017/eis.2018.3.

Bhambra, Gurminder K. 2017. 'The Current Crisis of Europe: Refugees, Colonialism, and the Limits of Cosmopolitanism'. *European Law Journal : Review of European Law in Context* 23 (5): 395–405. https://doi.org/10.1111/eulj.12234.

Bigo, Didier. 2010. *Europe's 21st Century Challenge: Delivering Liberty*. Farnham: Ashgate.

———. 2016. 'Frontiers of Fear: Immigration and Insecurity in the United States and Europe'. *Journal of Ethnic and Migration Studies: European Migration Governance since the Lisbon Treaty* 42 (4): 689–93. https://doi.org/10.1080/1369183X.2015.1123857.

———. 2017. 'International Flows, Political Order and Social Change: (In)Security, by-Product of the Will of Order Over Change'. *Global Crime* 18 (3): 303–21. https://doi.org/10.1080/17440572.2017.1350428.

Bilge, Sirma. 2008. '5. Between Gender and Cultural Equality'. *Recasting the Social in Citizenship* 100. https://www.academia.edu/1633447/Between_Gender_and_Cultural_Equality.

———. 2010. 'Beyond Subordination Vs. Resistance: An Intersectional Approach to the Agency of Veiled Muslim Women'. *Journal of Intercultural Studies* 31 (1): 9. https://www.academia.edu/235057/Beyond_Subordination_vs_Resistance_An_Intersectional_Approach_to_the_Agency_of_Veiled_Muslim_Women.

———. 2013. 'Reading the Racial Subtext of the Québécois Accommodation Controversy: An Analytics of Racialized Governmentality'. *Politikon* 40 (1): 157–81. https://doi.org/10.1080/02589346.2013.765681.

———. 2020. 'The Fungibility of Intersectionality: An Afropessimist Reading'. *Ethnic and Racial Studies* 43 (13): 2298–2326. https://doi.org/10.1080/01419870.2020.1740289.

Bilgin, Pinar. 2010. 'The "Western-Centrism" of Security Studies: "Blind Spot" or Constitutive Practice?' *Security Dialogue* 41 (6): 615–22. https://doi.org/10.1177/0967010610388208.

———. 2011. 'The Politics of Studying Securitization? The Copenhagen School in Turkey'. *Security Dialogue* 42 (4/5): 399–412. https://doi.org/10.1177/0967010611418711.

Bobbio, Norberto. 2006. *The Age of Rights*. Cambridge, England: Polity Press.

Boltanski, Luc. 1999. *Distant Suffering: Morality, Media, and Politics. Cambridge Cultural Social Studies*. Cambridge: University Press.

Bordo, Susan. 2004. *Unbearable Weight: Feminism, Western Culture, and the Body*. University of California Press.

Bourdieu, Pierre. 1984. *Distinction: A Social Critique of the Judgement of Taste*. London: Routledge.

Brayson, Kimberley. 2019. 'Of Bodies and Burkinis: Institutional Islamophobia, Islamic Dress, and the Colonial Condition'. *Journal of Law and Society* 46 (1): 55–82. https://doi.org/10.1111/jols.12142.

Brown, Katherine. 2006. 'Realising Muslim Women's Rights: The Role of Islamic Identity among British Muslim Women'. *Women's Studies International Forum, Islam, Gender and Human Rights* 29 (4): 417–30. https://doi.org/10.1016/j.wsif.2006.05.002.

Brown, Wendy. 2000. 'Suffering Rights as Paradoxes'. *Constellations* 7 (2): 208–29. https://doi.org/10.1111/1467-8675.00183.

———. 2011. 'Human Rights and the Politics of Fatalism'. *Wronging Rights?* India: Routledge.

———. 2012. 'Civilizational Delusions: Secularism, Tolerance, Equality'. *Theory & Event* 15 (2). https://muse.jhu.edu/pub/1/article/478356.

———. 2019. *In the Ruins of Neoliberalism: The Rise of Antidemocratic Politics in the West*. The Wellek Library Lectures. New York: Columbia University Press.

———. 2020. *States of Injury: Power and Freedom in Late Modernity*. Princeton, NJ: Princeton University Press.

Brown, Wendy, and Janet Halley, eds. 2002. *Left Legalism/Left Critique*. Durham, NC: Duke University Press.

Brown, Wendy, Janet Halley, Richard Thompson Ford, Lauren Berlant, Mark Kelman, and Gillian Lester. 2002. *Left Legalism/Left Critique.* Durham: Duke University Press. http://ebookcentral.proquest.com/lib/suss/detail.action?docID=1167804.

Burchardt, Marian, Zeynep Yanasmayan, and Matthias Koenig. 2019. 'The Judicial Politics of Burqa Bans in Belgium and Spain—Socio-Legal Field Dynamics and the Standardization of Justificatory Repertoires'. *Law & Social Inquiry* 44 (2): 333–58. https://doi.org/10.1111/lsi.12359.

Butler, Judith. 1995. 'Melancholy Gender-Refused Identification'. *Psychoanalytic Dialogues* 5 (2): 165–80. https://doi.org/10.1080/10481889509539059.

———. 2004. *Undoing Gender.* New York: Routledge.

———. 2012. 'Precarious Life, Vulnerability, and the Ethics of Cohabitation'. *The Journal of Speculative Philosophy* 26 (2): 134–51. https://doi.org/10.5325/jspecphil.26.2.0134.

Butler, Judith, Zeynep Gambetti, and Leticia Sabsay. 2016. *Vulnerability in Resistance.* Durham, NC: Duke University Press.

Butler, Michael J. 2020. *Securitization Revisited: Contemporary Applications and Insights* (1st ed., Vol. 1). Routledge Critical Security Studies. Milton: Routledge. https://doi.org/10.4324/9780429054648.

Buzan, Barry, Ole Wæver, and Jaap de Wilde. 1998. *Security: A New Framework for Analysis.* Lynne Rienner Publishers.

Calhoun, Craig J. 2002. 'The Class Consciousness of Frequent Travelers: Toward a Critique of Actually Existing Cosmopolitanism'. *The South Atlantic Quarterly* 101 (4): 869–97. https://muse.jhu.edu/pub/4/article/39104.

Camus, Albert. 1953. *The Rebel.* London: Hamilton.

Cheah, Pheng. 2006. *Inhuman Conditions: On Cosmopolitanism and Human Rights.* Cambridge, MA: Harvard University Press.

Côté, Adam. 2016. 'Agents Without Agency: Assessing the Role of the Audience in Securitization Theory'. *Security Dialogue* 47 (6): 541–58. https://doi.org/10.1177/0967010616672150.

Cronin, Audrey Kurth. 2002. 'Behind the Curve: Globalization and International Terrorism'. *International Security* 27 (3): 30–58. http://www.jstor.org/stable/3092113.

Cruz, Katie, and Wendy Brown. 2016a. 'Feminism, Law, and Neoliberalism: An Interview and Discussion With Wendy Brown'. *Feminist Legal Studies* 24 (1): 69–89. https://doi.org/10.1007/s10691-016-9314-z.

———. 2016b. 'Feminism, Law, and Neoliberalism: An Interview and Discussion with Wendy Brown'. *Feminist Legal Studies* 24 (1): 69–89. https://doi.org/10.1007/s10691-016-9314-z.

Davis, Muriam Haleh. 2011. '"A New World Rising": Albert Camus and the Absurdity of Neo-Liberalism'. *Social Identities* 17 (2): 225–38. https://doi.org/10.1080/13504630.2011.558375.

Dembour, Marie-Bénédicte. 2006. *Who Believes in Human Rights?: Reflections on the European Convention.* Cambridge, MA: Cambridge University Press.

Dencik, Lina, and Jonathan Cable. 2017. 'The Advent of Surveillance Realism: Public Opinion and Activist Responses to the Snowden Leaks'. *International Journal of Communication* 11 (November): 763–81. http://ijoc.org/index.php/ijoc/article/view/5524/1939.

Derrida, Jacques. 1998. *Monolingualism of the Other: Or, the Prosthesis of Origin.* Standford, CA: Stanford University Press.

Diken, Bülent, and Carsten Bagge Laustsen. 2005. 'Becoming Abject: Rape as a Weapon of War'. *Body & Society* 11 (1): 111–28. https://doi.org/10.1177/1357034X05049853.

Douzinas, Costas. 2000. *The End of Human Rights: Critical Legal Thought at the Turn of the Century*. Oxford: Hart.

———. 2013. 'The Paradoxes of Human Rights: The Paradox of Human Rights: Costas Douzinas'. *Constellations (Oxford, England)* 20 (1): 51–67. https://doi.org/10.1111/cons.12021.

Duara, Prasenjit. 2004. *Decolonization: Perspectives From Now and Then*. London: Routledge.

Duran, Javier. 2010. 'Virtual Borders, Data Aliens, and Bare Bodies: Culture, Securitization, and the Biometric State'. *Journal of Borderlands Studies* 25 (3–4): 219–30. https://doi.org/10.1080/08865655.2010.9695783.

Dzehtsiarou, Kanstantsin, and Alex Schwartz. 2020. 'Electing Team Strasbourg: Professional Diversity on the European Court of Human Rights and Why It Matters'. *German Law Journal* 21 (4): 621–43. https://doi.org/10.1017/glj.2020.36.

Edmunds, Aneira J. 2021. 'Precarious Bodies: The Securitization of the "Veiled" Woman in European Human Rights'. *The British Journal of Sociology* 72 (2): 315–27. https://doi.org/10.1111/1468-4446.12806.

Edwards, A. 2005. 'Human Rights, Refugees, and the Right "To Enjoy" Asylum'. *International Journal of Refugee Law* 17 (2): 293–330. https://doi.org/10.1093/ijrl/eei011.

Eisenman, Stephen. 2010. *The Abu Ghraib Effect*. London: Reaktion Books.

Entwistle, Joanne. 2020. 'Addressing the Body'. In *Fashion Theory* (2nd ed.). London: Routledge.

Fanon, Frantz. 2004. *The Wretched of the Earth / Frantz Fanon; Translated From the French by Richard Philcox hiIntroductions by Jean-Paul Sartre and Homi K. Bhabha*. New York: Grove Press.

———. 2021. *Black Skin, White Masks*. London: Penguin Classics.

Fernández, Belén. n.d. 'Rape as a Weapon of War Against Asylum Seekers'. Accessed 6 April 2023. https://www.aljazeera.com/opinions/2023/3/19/rape-as-a-weapon-in-the-war-on-asylum-seekers.

Fernando, Mayanthi L. 2009. 'Breaking the Silence: French Women's Voices From the Ghetto (Review)'. *JMEWS: Journal of Middle East Women's Studies* 5 (1): 97–100.

Fouladvand, Shahrzad. 2014a. 'Complementarity and Cultural Sensitivity: Decision-Making by the International Criminal Court Prosecutor in the Darfur Situation'. *International Criminal Law Review* 14 (6): 1028–66. https://doi.org/10.1163/15718123-01406003.

———. 2014b. 'Complementarity and Cultural Sensitivity: Decision-Making by the International Criminal Court Prosecutor in the Darfur Situation'. *International Criminal Law Review* 14 (6): 1028–66. https://doi.org/10.1163/15718123-01406003.

Fournier, Pascale. 2013. 'Headscarf and Burqa Controversies at the Crossroad of Politics, Society and Law'. *Social Identities* 19 (6): 689–703. https://doi.org/10.1080/13504630.2013.842669.

Galembert, Claire de, Matthias Koenig, and Sarah-Louise Raillard. 2014. 'Governing Religion With Judges: Introduction'. *Revue Française de Science Politique (English Edition)* 64 (4): 1–16. https://www.jstor.org/stable/revfranscipoleng.64.4.1.

Georgi, Richard. 2016. 'Human Rights Activism and the (De-)Securitization of the "Other"'. *Politikon: The IAPSS Journal of Political Science* 29 (March): 55–87. https://doi.org/10.22151/politikon.29.4.

Goffman, Erving. 1968. *Asylums: Essays on the Social Situation of Mental Patients and Other Inmates.* Harmondsworth: Penguin; Pelican Books.

Gokariksel, Banu, and Anna J. Secor. 2014. 'The Veil, Desire, and the Gaze: Turning the Inside Out'. *Signs: Journal of Women in Culture and Society,* September. https://www.academia.edu/8439581/The_Veil_Desire_and_the_Gaze_Turning_the_Inside_Out.

Gole, Nilufer. 2002. 'Islam in Public: New Visibilities and New Imaginaries'. *Public Culture* 14 (1): 173–90. http://muse.jhu.edu/article/26271.

———. 2003. 'The Voluntary Adoption of Islamic Stigma Symbols'. *Social Research: An International Quarterly* 70 (3): 809–28. https://doi.org/10.1353/sor.2003.0005.

———. 2011. 'The Public Visibility of Islam and European Politics of Resentment: The Minarets-Mosques Debate'. *Philosophy & Social Criticism* 37 (4): 383–92. https://doi.org/10.1177/0191453711398773.

———. 2012. 'Decentering Europe, Recentering Islam'. *New Literary History* 43 (4): 665–85. https://doi.org/10.1353/nlh.2012.0041.

———. 2017a. 'Turkey is Undergoing a Radical Shift, From Pluralism to Islamic Populism'. *New Perspectives Quarterly* 34 (4): 45–49. https://doi.org/10.1111/npqu.12109.

———. 2017b. *The Daily Lives of Muslims: Islam and Public Confrontation in Contemporary Europe.* London: Zed Books Ltd.

Goodale, Mark. 2022. *Reinventing Human Rights.* Stanford, CA: Stanford University Press.

Graham, Luke D. 2022. 'The Right to Clothing and Personal Protective Equipment in the Context of COVID-19'. *The International Journal of Human Rights* 26 (1): 30–49. https://doi.org/10.1080/13642987.2021.1874939.

Grear, Anna. 2006. 'Human Rights – Human Bodies? Some Reflections on Corporate Human Rights Distortion, the Legal Subject, Embodiment and Human Rights Theory'. *Law and Critique* 17 (2): 171–99. https://doi.org/10.1007/s10978-006-0006-8.

———. 2007. 'Challenging Corporate "Humanity": Legal Disembodiment, Embodiment and Human Rights'. *Human Rights Law Review* 7 (3): 511–43. https://doi.org/10.1093/hrlr/ngm013.

———. 2015. 'Deconstructing Anthropos: A Critical Legal Reflection on "Anthropocentric" Law and Anthropocene "Humanity"'. *Law and Critique* 26 (3): 225–49. https://doi.org/10.1007/s10978-015-9161-0.

Grosz, Elizabeth. 1994. *Volatile Bodies: Toward a Corporeal Feminism. Theories of Representation and Difference.* Bloomington: Indiana University Press.

Guardiola-Rivera, Óscar. 2010. *What If Latin America Ruled the World?: How the South Will Take the North Through the 21st Century* (1st U.S. ed.). New York: Bloomsbury Press.

———. 2017. 'Concerning Violence, Part 1: The People Are Missing'. *Discourse* 39 (2): 155–76. https://doi.org/10.13110/discourse.39.2.0155.

Guénif-Souilamas, Nacira. 2006. 'The Other French Exception: Virtuous Racism and the War of the Sexes in Postcolonial France'. *French Politics, Culture & Society* 24 (3): 23–41. http://www.jstor.org/stable/42843464.

Habermas, Jurgen. 1991. *The Structural Transformation of the Public Sphere: An Inquiry into a Category of Bourgeois Society.* Cambridge, MA: MIT Press.

Hafez, Farid. 2014. 'Shifting Borders: Islamophobia as Common Ground for Building Pan-European Right-Wing Unity'. *Patterns of Prejudice* 48 (5): 479–99. https://doi.org/10.1080/0031322X.2014.965877.

Hansen, Lene. 2011. 'Theorizing the Image for Security Studies: Visual Securitization and the Muhammad Cartoon Crisis*'. *European Journal of International Relations* 17 (1): 51–74. https://doi.org/10.1177/1354066110388593.

Hansen, Lene.2020.'Are "Core" Feminist Critiques of Securitization Theory Racist? A Reply to Alison Howell and Melanie Richter-Montpetit'. *Security Dialogue*51(4):378–385. https://doi.org/10.1177/0967010620907198.

Hayden, Patrick. 2013. 'Albert Camus and Rebellious Cosmopolitanism in a Divided Worlda'. *Journal of International Political Theory* 9 (2): 194–219. https://doi.org/10.3366 /jipt.2013.0055.

Heck, Axel, and Gabi Schlag. 2013. 'Securitizing Images: The Female Body and the War in Afghanistan'. *European Journal of International Relations* 19 (4): 891–913. https://doi .org/10.1177/1354066111433896.

Heindl, Brett S. 2017. 'Muslim Immigration and Religious Human Rights'. *International Politics (Hague, Netherlands)* 54 (1): 26–42. https://doi.org/10.1057/s41311-017-0016-1.

Hekman, Susan.2000.'Beyond Identity: Feminism, Identity and Identity Politics'.*Feminist Theory*1(3):289–308. https://doi.org/10.1177/14647000022229245.

Hirschauer, S. 2014. *The Securitization of Rape: Women, War and Sexual Violence*. London: Palgrave Macmillan UK. http://ebookcentral.proquest.com/lib/suss/detail.action ?docID=1952986.

Hirschl, Ran. 2008. 'The Judicialization of Politics'. In *The Oxford Handbook of Law and Politics*, edited by Gregory A. Caldeira, R. Daniel Kelemen, and Keith E. Whittington. Oxford: Oxford University Press. https://doi.org/10.1093/oxfordhb/9780199208425 .003.0008.

Hübinette, Tobias, and Catrin Lundström.2011.'Sweden after the Recent Election: The Double-Binding Power of Swedish Whiteness Through the Mourning of the Loss of "Old Sweden" and the Passing of "Good Sweden"'.*NORA - Nordic Journal of Feminist and Gender Research*19(1):42–52. https://doi.org/10.1080/08038740.2010 .547835.

Huysmans, Jef. 2005. *The Politics of Insecurity: Fear, Migration and Asylum in the EU*. London: Routledge.

———. 2014. *Security Unbound: Enacting Democratic Limits*. London: Routledge.

Ibrahim, Maggie. 2005. 'The Securitization of Migration: A Racial Discourse'. *International Migration* 43 (5): 163–87. https://doi.org/10.1111/j.1468-2435.2005.00345 .x.

Isin, Engin F., and Greg Marc Nielsen. 2008. *Acts of Citizenship*. London: Zed Books Ltd.

Jonker, Gerdien, and Valérie Amiraux. 2015. *Politics of Visibility Young Muslims in European Public Spaces* (1st ed.). Globaler Lokaler Islam. Bielefeld: Transcript Verlag. https://doi .org/10.14361/9783839405062.

Krasteva, Anna. 2017. 'Editorial of Special Focus: Securitisation and Its Impact on Human Rights and Human Security'.

———. 2020. 'If Borders Did Not Exist, Euroscepticism Would Have Invented Them Or, on Post-Communist Re/De/Re/Bordering in Bulgaria'. *Geopolitics* 25 (3): 678–705. https://doi.org/10.1080/14650045.2017.1398142.

Kratochvíl, Jan. 2011. 'The Inflation of the Margin of Appreciation by the European Court of Human Rights'. *Netherlands Quarterly of Human Rights* 29 (3): 324–57. https:// doi.org/10.1177/016934411102900304.

Kreide, Regina. 2015. 'Human Rights as Placeholders'. *Fudan Journal of the Humanities and Social Sciences* 8 (3): 401–13. https://doi.org/10.1007/s40647-015-0093-8.

———. 2019. 'Crossing (Out) Borders: Human Rights and the Securitization of Roma Minorities'. In *The Securitization of the Roma in Europe*, edited by Huub van Baar, Ana Ivasiuc, and Regina Kreide, 45–66. Human Rights Interventions. Cham: Springer International Publishing. https://doi.org/10.1007/978-3-319-77035-2_3.

Kurban, Dilek. 2020. *Limits of Supranational Justice: The European Court of Human Rights and Turkey's Kurdish Conflict*. Cambridge, MA: Cambridge University Press.

Kymlicka, Will, and Keith G. Banting. 2006. *Multiculturalism and the Welfare State: Recognition and Redistribution in Contemporary Democracies*. Oxford: Oxford University Press.

Laborde, Cécile. 2012. 'State Paternalism and Religious Dress Code'. *International Journal of Constitutional Law* 10 (2): 398–410. https://doi.org/10.1093/icon/mor059.

Lazreg, Marnia. 2016. *Torture and the Twilight of Empire: From Algiers to Baghdad. Torture and the Twilight of Empire*. Princeton, NJ: Princeton University Press. https://doi.org/10.1515/9781400883813.

Leckey, Robert. 2013. 'Face to Face'. *Social Identities* 19 (6): 743–58. https://doi.org/10.1080/13504630.2013.842672.

Legros, Olivier, and Marion Lièvre. 2019. 'Domestic Versus State Reason? How Roma Migrants in France Deal With Their Securitization'. In *The Securitization of the Roma in Europe*, edited by Huub van Baar, Ana Ivasiuc, and Regina Kreide, 67–87. Human Rights Interventions. Cham: Springer International Publishing. https://doi.org/10.1007/978-3-319-77035-2_4.

Livingston, Steven, and Mathias Risse. 2019. 'The Future Impact of Artificial Intelligence on Humans and Human Rights'. *Ethics & International Affairs* 33 (2): 141–58. https://doi.org/10.1017/S089267941900011X.

Lorasdagi, Berrin Koyuncu. 2009. 'The Headscarf and 'Resistance Identity-Building': A Case Study on Headscarf-Wearing in Amsterdam'. *Women's Studies International Forum* 32(6):453–463. https://doi.org/10.1016/j.wsif.2009.09.008.

MacKinnon, Catharine A. 2007. *Women's Lives, Men's Laws*. Cambridge, MA: Belknap.

Madsen, Mikael Rask. 2018. 'Rebalancing European Human Rights: Has the Brighton Declaration Engendered a New Deal on Human Rights in Europe?' *Journal of International Dispute Settlement* 9 (2): 199–222. https://doi.org/10.1093/jnlids/idx016.

Mahmood, Saba. 2001. 'Feminist Theory, Embodiment, and the Docile Agent: Some Reflections on the Egyptian Islamic Revival'. *Cultural Anthropology* 16 (2): 202–36. http://www.jstor.org/stable/656537.

Mahmood, Saba, and Saba Mahmood. 2011. *Politics of Piety: The Islamic Revival and the Feminist Subject* (Rev-revised). Princeton, NJ: Princeton University Press.

Mayer, Tamar. 2000. *Gender Ironies of Nationalism: Sexing the Nation*. London: Routledge.

Mbembe, Achille. 2017. *Critique of Black Reason*. Durham, NC: Duke University Press.

Mejia, Silvia. 2021. 'Disposable Bodies: Undocumented Migrants and Lajaula de Oro's Poetics of Austerity'. *Latin American Literary Review* 48 (96): 86.

Mill, John Stuart. 1949. 'On the Liberty of Thought and Discussion [1859]'. In *Primer of Intellectual Freedom*, edited by Howard Mumford Jones, 110–141. Cambridge London: Harvard University Press. https://doi.org/10.4159/harvard.9780674367296.c12.

Morsut, Claudia, and Bjørn Ivar Kruke. 2018. 'Crisis Governance of the Refugee and Migrant Influx into Europe in 2015: A Tale of Disintegration'. *Journal of European Integration* 40 (2): 145–59. https://doi.org/10.1080/07036337.2017.1404055.

Motha, Stewart. 2007. 'Veiled Women and the Affect of Religion in Democracy'. *Journal of Law and Society* 34 (1): 139–62. https://doi.org/10.1111/j.1467-6478.2007.00386.x.

Moyn, Samuel. 2012. *The Last Utopia: Human Rights in History*. Cambridge, MA: Harvard University Press.

———. 2018. *Not Enough: Human Rights in an Unequal World*. Cambridge, MA: The Belknap Press of Harvard University Press.

Muller, Benjamin J. 2004. '(Dis)Qualified Bodies: Securitization, Citizenship and "Identity Management"'. *Citizenship Studies* 8 (3): 279–94. https://doi.org/10.1080/1362102042000257005.

Nash, Kate. 2007. 'The Pinochet Case: Cosmopolitanism and Intermestic Human Rights'. *The British Journal of Sociology* 58 (3): 417–35. https://doi.org/10.1111/j.1468-4446.2007.00158.x.

———. 2009. 'Between Citizenship and Human Rights'. *Sociology* 43 (6): 1067–83. http://www.jstor.org/stable/42857339.

———. 2012. 'Human Rights, Movements and Law: On Not Researching Legitimacy'. *Sociology (Oxford)* 46 (5): 797–812. https://doi.org/10.1177/0038038512451528.

———. 2016. 'Politicising Human Rights in Europe: Challenges to Legal Constitutionalism From the Left and the Right'. *The International Journal of Human Rights* 20 (8): 1295–1308. https://doi.org/10.1080/13642987.2016.1239616.

———. 2019. 'The Cultural Politics of Human Rights and Neoliberalism'. *Journal of Human Rights* 18 (5): 490–505. https://doi.org/10.1080/14754835.2019.1653174.

Nuñez-Mietz, Fernando G. 2019. 'Resisting Human Rights Through Securitization: Russia and Hungary Against LGBT Rights'. *Journal of Human Rights* 18 (5): 543–63. https://doi.org/10.1080/14754835.2019.1647100.

Nussbaum, Martha C. 2005. 'Women's Bodies: Violence, Security, Capabilities'. *Journal of Human Development* 6 (2): 167–83. https://doi.org/10.1080/14649880500120509.

Nyers, Peter. 2003. 'Abject Cosmopolitanism: The Politics of Protection in the Anti-Deportation Movement'. *Third World Quarterly* 24 (6): 1069–93. http://www.jstor.org/stable/3993444.

Ochab, Ewelina U. n.d. 'Behind the Camps' Gates: Rape and Sexual Violence Against Uyghur Women'. *Forbes*. Accessed 6 April 2023. https://www.forbes.com/sites/ewelinaochab/2021/02/03/behind-the-camps-gates-rape-and-sexual-violence-against-uyghur-women/.

Owens, Patricia. 2017. 'Racism in the Theory Canon: Hannah Arendt and "the One Great Crime in Which America Was Never Involved"'. *Millennium* 45 (3): 403–24. https://doi.org/10.1177/0305829817695880.

Pereira-Ares, Noemí. 2017. *Fashion, Dress and Identity in South Asian Diaspora Narratives: From the Eighteenth Century to Monica Ali*. Cham:Springer International Publishing AG. https://doi.org/10.1007/978-3-319-61397-0.

Petrov, Jan. 2020. 'The Populist Challenge to the European Court of Human Rights'. *International Journal of Constitutional Law* 18 (2): 476–508. https://doi.org/10.1093/icon/moaa027.

Puar, Jasbir K. 2017. *The Right to Maim: Debility, Capacity, Disability*. Anima. Durham: Duke University Press.

Razack, Sherene. 2008. *Casting Out: The Eviction of Muslims From Western Law and Politics*. Toronto: University of Toronto Press.

Reid, Donald. 2007. 'The Worlds of Frantz Fanon's "L'Algérie Se Dévoile"'. *French Studies* 61 (4): 460–75. https://doi.org/10.1093/fs/knm128.

Risse, Mathias. 2019. 'Human Rights and Artificial Intelligence: An Urgently Needed Agenda'. *Human Rights Quarterly* 41: 1. https://heinonline.org/HOL/Page?handle=hein.journals/hurq41&id=7&div=&collection=.

Rorive, Isabelle. 2008. 'Religious Symbols in the Public Space: In Search of a European Answer'. *Cardozo Law Review* 30: 2669. https://heinonline.org/HOL/Page?handle=hein.journals/cdozo30&id=2687&div=&collection=.

Roth, Kenneth. 2017. 'The Dangerous Rise of Populism: Global Attacks on Human Rights Values'. *Journal of International Affairs*, 79–84. http://www.jstor.org/stable/44842604.

Sabsay, Leticia. 2012. 'The Emergence of the Other Sexual Citizen: Orientalism and the Modernisation of Sexuality'. *Citizenship Studies* 16 (5–6): 605–23. https://doi.org/10.1080/13621025.2012.698484.

———. 2020. 'The Political Aesthetics of Vulnerability and the Feminist Revolt'. *Critical Times* 3 (2): 179–99. https://doi.org/10.1215/26410478-8517711.

Said, Edward W. 1979. *Orientalism* (1st ed.). New York: Vintage Books.

———. 1999. *Out of Place: A Memoir*. London: Granta Books.

Salter, Mark B. 2008. 'Securitization and Desecuritization: A Dramaturgical Analysis of the Canadian Air Transport Security Authority'. *Journal of International Relations and Development* 11 (4): 321–49. https://doi.org/10.1057/jird.2008.20.

Samson, Colin. 2020. *The Colonialism of Human Rights: Ongoing Hypocrisies of Western Liberalism*. New York: John Wiley & Sons.

Santos, Boaventura de Sousa, and Santos Boaventura. 2015. *If God Were a Human Rights Activist*. Stanford Studies in Human Rights. Palo Alto: Stanford University Press.

Scheingold, Stuart A. 2010. *The Politics of Rights: Lawyers, Public Policy, and Political Change*. Ann Arbor: University of Michigan Press.

Shafak, Elif. 2020. *10 Minutes 38 Seconds in This Strange World*. London: Penguin Books.

Shamir, Ronen. 2005. 'Without Borders? Notes on Globalization as a Mobility Regime*'. *Sociological Theory* 23 (2): 197–217. https://doi.org/10.1111/j.0735-2751.2005.00250.x.

Skeet, Charlotte. 2009. 'Globalisation of Women's Rights Norms: The Right to Manifest Religion and Orientalism in the Council of Europe'. *Public Space: The Journal of Law and Social Justice* 4: 34. https://heinonline.org/HOL/Page?handle=hein.journals/pubspac4&id=34&div=&collection=.

Soysal, Yasemin Nuhoglu. 1995. *Limits of Citizenship: Migrants and Postnational Membership in Europe*. Chicago, IL: University of Chicago Press.

Steinbach, Armin.2015.'Burqas and Bans Armin Steinbach Burqas and Bans: The Wearing of Religious Symbols under the European Convention of Human Rights Cambridge'.*Journal of International and Comparative Law*4(1). https://doi.org/10.7574/cjicl.04.01.29.

Stonebridge, Lyndsey. 2021. *Writing and Righting: Literature in the Age of Human Rights* (1st ed.). Oxford, UK: Oxford University Press.

Stritzel, Holger. 2007. 'Towards a Theory of Securitization: Copenhagen and Beyond'. *European Journal of International Relations* 13 (3): 357–83. https://doi.org/10.1177/1354066107080128.

Táíwò, Olúfẹ́mi.2022.*Against Decolonisation: Taking African Agency Seriously Hurst*.London. Hurst Publishers.

Triandafyllidou, Anna. 2011. *European Multiculturalisms: Cultural, Religious and Ethnic Challenges*. Edinburgh, NJ: Edinburgh University Press.

Turner, Bryan S. 1993. 'Outline of a Theory of Human Rights'. *Sociology (Oxford)* 27 (3): 489–512. https://doi.org/10.1177/0038038593027003009.

———. 2001a. *Society and Culture: Principles of Scarcity and Solidarity*. Theory, Culture & Society. London: SAGE.

———. 2001b. 'The Erosion of Citizenship'. *The British Journal of Sociology* 52 (2): 189–209. https://doi.org/10.1080/00071310120044944.

———. 2002. 'Cosmopolitan Virtue, Globalization and Patriotism'. *Theory, Culture & Society* 19 (1–2): 45–63. https://doi.org/10.1177/0263276402019001003.

————. 2006. *Vulnerability and Human Rights: Essays on Human Rights*. State College: Pennsylvania State University Press. https://doi.org/10.5325/j.ctt7v124.

————. 2007. 'The Enclave Society: Towards a Sociology of Immobility'. *European Journal of Social Theory* 10 (2): 287–304. https://doi.org/10.1177/1368431007077807.

————. 2008. *The Body & Society: Explorations in Social Theory* (3rd ed.). Theory, Culture & Society. Los Angeles, CA: SAGE.

————. 2011. *Religion and Modern Society: Citizenship, Secularisation and the State*. Cambridge: Cambridge University Press.

————. 2016. 'We Are All Denizens Now: On the Erosion of Citizenship'. *Citizenship Studies* 20 (6–7): 679–92. https://doi.org/10.1080/13621025.2016.1191432.

Turner, Bryan S., and Chris Rojek. 2001. *Society and Culture: Scarcity and Solidarity*. London: SAGE.

Turner, Bryan S., and June Edmunds. 2002. 'The Distaste of Taste: Bourdieu, Cultural Capital and the Australian Postwar Elite'. *Journal of Consumer Culture* 2 (2): 219–39. https://doi.org/10.1177/146954050200200204.

Turner, Terence S. 2012. 'The Social Skin'. *HAU: Journal of Ethnographic Theory* 2 (2): 486–504. https://doi.org/10.14318/hau2.2.026.

Tzelepis, Elena. 2016. '7 Vulnerable Corporealities and Precarious Belongings in Mona Hatoum's Art'. In *7 Vulnerable Corporealities and Precarious Belongings in Mona Hatoum's Art*, 146–66. Durham, NC: Duke University Press. https://doi.org/10.1515/9780822373490-010.

Voeten, Erik. 2007. 'The Politics of International Judicial Appointments: Evidence From the European Court of Human Rights'. *International Organization* 61 (4): 669–701. http://www.jstor.org/stable/4498164.

————. 2008. 'The Impartiality of International Judges: Evidence From the European Court of Human Rights'. *American Political Science Review* 102 (4): 417–33. https://doi.org/10.1017/S0003055408080398.

Welborne, Bozena C., Aubrey L. Westfall, Özge Çelik Russell, and Sarah A. Tobin. 2018. *The Politics of the Headscarf in the United States*. Ithaca, NY: Cornell University Press. https://www.jstor.org/stable/10.7591/j.cttlw0dd2b.

Williams, Michael C. 2011. 'Securitization and the Liberalism of Fear'. *Security Dialogue* 42 (4–5): 453–63. https://doi.org/10.1177/0967010611418717.

Yılmaz, Ferruh. 2012. 'Right-Wing Hegemony and Immigration: How the Populist Far-Right Achieved Hegemony Through the Immigration Debate in Europe'. *Current Sociology* 60 (3): 368–81. https://doi.org/10.1177/0011392111426192.

INDEX

Note: Page locators followed by 'n' refer to notes.

Printed in the USA
CPSIA information can be obtained
at www.ICGtesting.com
JSHW020906051123
51488JS00001B/1